The Workbook of Photo Techniques

John Hedgecoe

The Workbook of Photo Techniques

Focal Press is an imprint of Butterworth–Heinemann.

Copyright © 1997 by Butterworth–Heinemann

 A member of the Reed Elsevier group

All rights reserved.

Recognizing the importance of preserving what has been written,
Butterworth–Heinemann prints its books on acid-free paper whenever possible.

© 1985, 1997 Reed International Books Ltd
Text © 1985, 1997 Reed International Books Ltd and John Hedgecoe
Photographs © 1978, 1979, 1980, 1982, 1983, 1984, and 1997 John Hedgecoe
Reprinted 1985, 1986
First paperback edition 1990, reprinted 1994
Revised and updated 1997

Typeset by Dorchester Typesetting Group Ltd, Dorchester, Dorset, England

Editor	Frank Wallis
Associate author	Richard Platt
Consultant art editor	Mel Petersen
Art Editor	Zoe Davenport
Production	Jean Rigby
Artist	Kuo Kang Chen

Revised edition	
Contributing editor	Chris George
Senior editor	Penelope Cream
Editor	Cathy Lowne
Production controller	Rachel Lynch

Executive editor	Judith More
Executive art editor	Janis Utton

Additional photographs © Stephen Dalton/Oxford Scientific Films pp 72-73; Fred Dustin p 128.

ISBN 0-240-80323-X

The publisher offers special discounts on bulk orders of this book.
For information, please contact:
Manager of Special Sales
Butterworth–Heinemann
225 Wildwood Avenue
Woburn, MA 01801-2041
Tel: 617-928-2500
Fax: 617-928-2620

For information on all Focal Press publications available, contact our World Wide Web home page at:
http://www.bh.com/focalpress

10 9 8 7 6 5 4 3 2 1
Printed in China

The Workbook of Photo Techniques

John Hedgecoe

Focal Press
Boston • Oxford • Johannesburg • Melbourne • New Delhi • Singapore

CONTENTS

Introduction

Today's modern cameras have removed from photography much of the technical guesswork of the past. Focusing and exposure are now handled accurately and automatically by many cameras. What they cannot do, however, is replace the human input. They cannot choose your subject or scene, or decide how to capture it in the most convincing way. They cannot

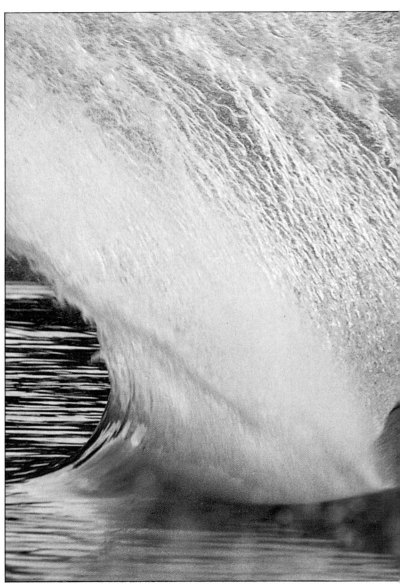

make decisions about what lens or viewpoint to use, or how to compose your picture. The camera is still only a highly efficient tool, and it needs skill to make proper use of it. This book is about how to do that; how to use equipment to its best advantage; how to make the decisions that you alone must make if you want to create not merely good photographs but great ones.

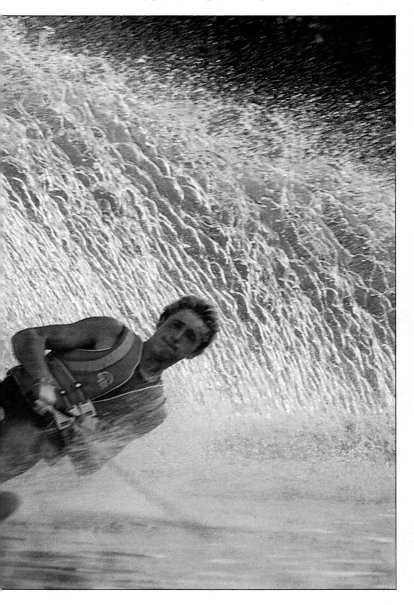

Get the Exposure Right

Film gives its best only when it receives a precisely regulated amount of light. The shutter speed and aperture controls work together to achieve this – but to set these controls, you must first measure how brightly the subject is lit. Most cameras now do this, but if you understand the principles of exposure, you can get better results, even with an automatic camera.

● **Know your meter.** The metering system on most modern SLRs takes readings from many different points across the image and biases the results based on 'typical exposures' that have been built into its memory. The matrix system is meant to eliminate most errors, but, in fact, makes it harder for the photographer to know when the camera is going to get it wrong.

● **Meter the most important area.** Avoid allowing your camera to be distracted by irrelevant bright or dark areas. Move or zoom in closer to the subject and take exposure readings. Remember the automatically selected shutter speed and aperture, reframe the picture as you want it, then adjust the manual mode to your predetermined settings.

● **Watch for false readings.** All meters assume that the subject is an average grey tone and will give incorrect results with light and dark subjects. With a light subject, you should open up one or two stops more than recommended by the meter, and vice versa.

● **Take care in sunlight.** On grey days, careless metering often does not matter, but sunny weather creates greater contrast.

● **Use a hand-held meter** with colour slide film. Transparencies need accurate light measurements and a hand-held meter can measure the light falling on the subject, a more accurate method than measuring reflected light.

● **Bracket exposures with slide film.** Take one picture at the indicated exposure, then over- and underexpose by half or one stop. This ensures that one of the three pictures will be perfectly exposed.

● **Measure incident light.** Incident light is the light that falls on the subject rather than that reflected from it. Measuring incident light is a way of increasing exposure accuracy. You need a hand-held meter with a diffuser over the light cell and to get the reading the meter should be pointed at the light source, not at the subject itself.

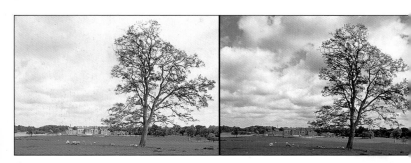

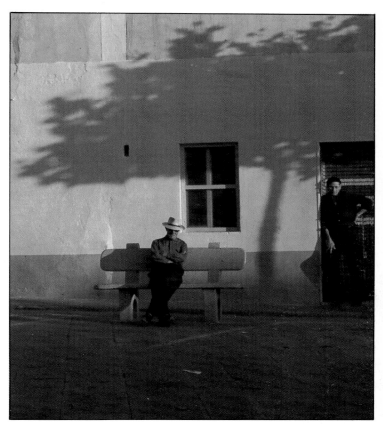

▲ A simple through-the-lens meter reading could easily result in the shadows being underexposed in a scene like this. Correct exposure is midway between a reading for the shadows and one for the highlights; here I used a 50mm lens at 1/50, f11.

▼ Only the aperture was changed to shoot the sequence below. The first shot, taken at f2.8, is overexposed, while the last (at f16) is too dark. The changing light, however, has meant that the centre pair, taken at f5.6 and f11 are both 'correct'.

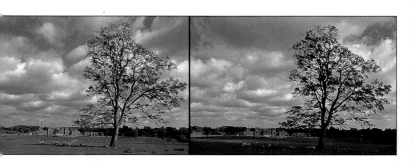

Balance the Controls

The camera's shutter speed and aperture do not just affect exposure. The shutter speed controls how movement appears on film, and the size of the aperture dictates how much of the picture will be sharp. So how do you balance the controls against each other for the best result?

● **Think ahead.** Do you want to blur movement? Or would you rather keep it sharp? Is it essential that the whole image is in focus, or would a blurred foreground improve the composition? Unless you weigh up all of these factors, you will not be able to make a reasoned decision about how to set each control.

● **Select shutter speed first** when you want to control the appearance of movement, as I did with the snowboarder on the opposite page. This can be done by using the exposure modes that your camera might have available – including metered manual, program shift, aperture priority and shutter priority. Whichever you find suits you best, the key is to change to the shutter speed that will avoid camera shake, or will convey the movement of the subject in the way that you want it.

● **Select aperture first** when you want to control depth of field. Wide apertures (low *f* numbers on the aperture ring) keep less of the subject sharp (see page 15). Small apertures (which, confusingly, have larger *f* numbers) give greater depth of field. Again, whichever of the exposure

modes you use, you should ensure that the aperture readout is at the setting you require.

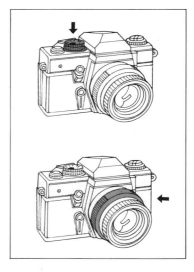

▼ A slow shutter speed helps to convey a sense of movement. A shutter speed of 1/4 was used: the people's movement has created very different pictures.

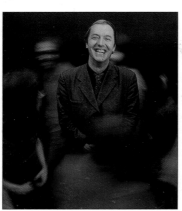

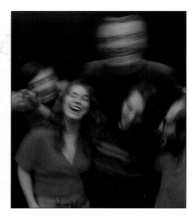

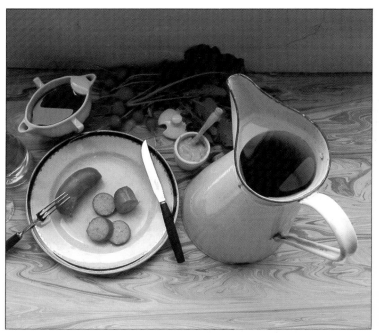

▲ Aperture was the important control in the still life – with the camera on a tripod,I exposed for one second and used *f*22 for maximum sharpness.

▼ Shutter speed had priority in the picture of the snowboarder: a 1/200 exposure ensured that he appeared sharp as he moved across the frame.

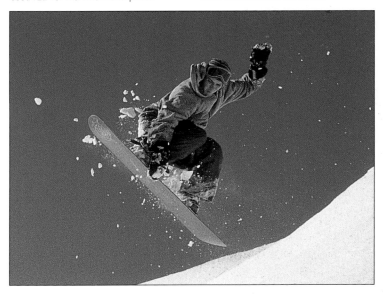

Use Exposure Latitude

Exposure errors are not always disastrous – you can sometimes compensate when making a print from the slide or negative. However, slide film is much more demanding than print film, which can be overexposed by several stops with little visible effect.

● **Use colour negative film** or black-and-white film – they have wide exposure latitude, which means that you do not have to spend too much time worrying about the accuracy of your meter.

● **Overexpose negative films** if you are unsure about the correct setting. With colour negative film and dye-image black-and-white film, overexposure actually has the effect of reducing grain size.

● **Colour transparency film** has very little exposure latitude. If anything, underexpose very slightly, because colours will be strengthened. You can rescue underexposed slides in printing.

▼ The larger picture was exposed for the bright sky, turning the foreground to shadow. For a more dreamy mood (below) I exposed for the shadowy trees to overexpose the sky and water.

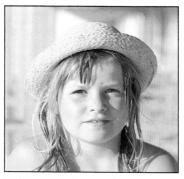

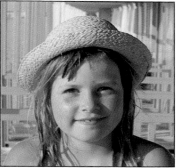

▲ Exposure for the girl's skin (1/125, *f*8) captured the sun. I closed down to *f*11 to increase sharpness and contrast.

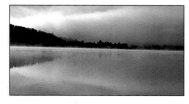

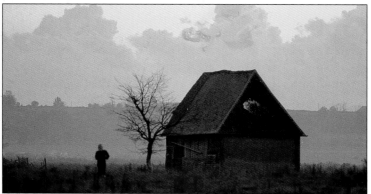

Vary Exposure for Tone

The exposure setting that your meter indicates is simply a guideline to follow rather than a never-to-be-broken rule. Often deliberate over- or underexposure will give equally good or even better results than if you slavishly follow the meter reading.

● **Use slide film** when aiming for precise control of tones. The laboratories that print colour negatives always compensate automatically for over- or underexposure, thus masking deliberate exposure changes that you might have made.

● **Overexpose for high-key.** Extra exposure will lighten and 'clean up' skin tones in a portrait, or suggest heat and brilliant sunlight in a landscape photograph.

● **Underexpose for low-key.** Tones will be darkened and colours will look richer. Outdoors, slight underexposure for a sombre mood can conjure up a storm even on a pleasant day and make rainy weather look like a thunderstorm.

▼ In high-contrast scenes there is rarely one correct exposure. I could have exposed for the dark skyscrapers, or the bright moody sky – instead I have biased the exposure towards the colourful flowers in the foreground.

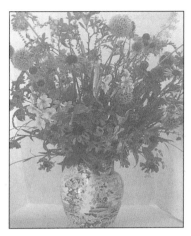

▲ By deliberately overexposing this shot of a floral display, I have ended up with a high-key result where the colours of the flowers have been rendered more mute than in reality. The bright white background adds a dreamy, ethereal quality to the still life.

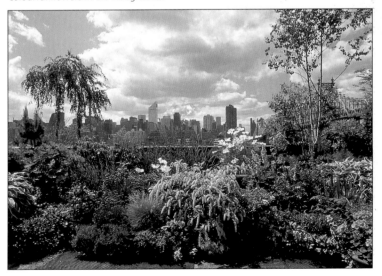

Focus Accurately

If you are using a shutter speed that is fast enough to rule out camera shake, or to freeze a moving subject, and your pictures still are not sharp, then (assuming the lens is in good condition) it is almost certain that your focusing is not sufficiently accurate.

● **Be decisive.** Turn the focusing ring quickly past the point of sharp focus, then back again until the picture is sharp. Then stop – and take the picture.

● **Move the camera to focus** to take close-ups. Depth of field is very shallow at short distances, and the quickest way to focus a hand-held camera is to move gently in and out. Once the subject is sharp, press the shutter release.

● **Use autofocus carefully.** Although AF systems are accurate, you do have to point the autofocus sensor area at the bit of the subject that you want in focus. You should still check visually for accurate focusing and, if necessary, revert to manual focusing.

● **Have a sight test!** Over half of all adults have defective vision, so glasses or contact lenses may well improve your pictures. You can fit a correction lens to the viewfinder window of your camera.

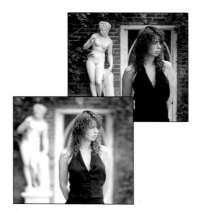

▲ When photographing people, focus on their eyes as this is the most important feature to get sharp.

▼ To focus on the legs of this girl sitting on a bench on the beach. I knelt down, focused approximately and leaned slowly forward to get the exact focus.

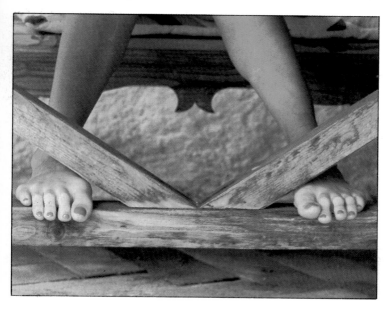

Exploit Depth of Field

Control of how large an area of the picture is sharp is one of the most valuable of photographic techniques that you can acquire: it enables you to draw attention to just one small part of a scene, or to record every detail of the subject with equal fidelity.

To expand the depth of field for overall clarity:

● **Stop down the lens.** Small apertures give more depth of field.

● **Use a wide-angle lens.** The shorter the focal length, the greater area of sharpness.

● **Focus a third to midway** between near and far points of the scene, then stop the lens down.

To reduce the depth of field and concentrate the attention on either the foreground or background:

● **Use the widest aperture.** In brilliant sunlight you may have to use slow film (or a dark grey neutral density filter).

● **Move close in.** Depth of field is less at short camera-to-subject distances.

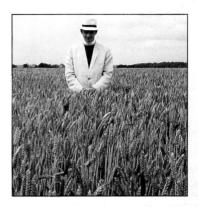

▲ The eye skips from the focused ears of wheat to the distant trees thanks to a wide-angle (35mm) lens at *f*22.

▼ The boy in the foreground dominates this picture – background detail and colour have been subdued by opening up to *f*5.6.

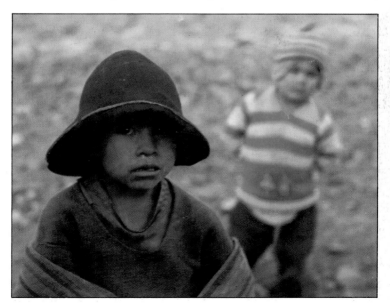

Select the Lens you Need

A photographer no longer needs five or six lenses for a variety of ways to tackle a subject: one or two zoom lenses will do. Normal lenses (50mm for 35mm film) approximate most closely to the view seen by the human eye. Lenses that give a greater angle of view are known as wide-angles, while those with a narrower, more selective field are called telephotos.

● **Use a wide-angle lens** for interiors, landscapes, and to add drama to mundane subjects. Wide-angle lenses make nearby subjects look bigger and shrink distant ones, exaggerating perspective. Depth of field is greater with shorter focal lengths.

● **Choose telephotos** to magnify the subject – for wildlife, sports, candid shots of children or people at work, and unselfconscious portraits. Telephotos can seem to compress perspective, bringing together subjects that are actually far apart.

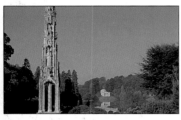

With wide-angle lenses, focusing becomes less critical, because the depth of field is so extensive.

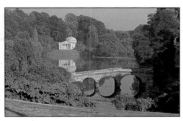

Normal lens settings (generally 50mm) offer the angle of view closest in focus to that seen by the human eye.

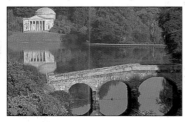

A long-focus lens brings distant subjects closer. But longer lenses have shallow depth of field.

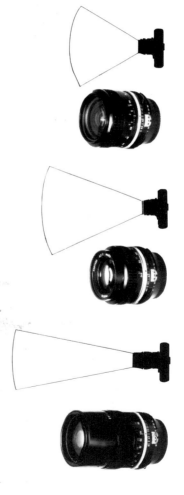

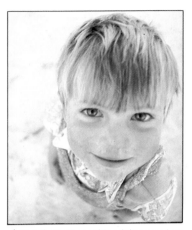

▲ The distortion in this adult's-eye view of a child has helped to create an arresting image, with the eyes at the centre point providing a direct contact that offsets the exaggeration of the head. Choose the angle of view carefully and, for close-ups, limit the lens to a medium wide-angle; ultra-wide lenses give unacceptable distortion. Here I used a 28mm lens.

▶ A 'normal' lens setting and a child's-eye viewpoint have given a natural-looking result.

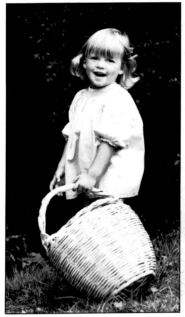

▼ A short telephoto setting enabled me to fill the frame to capture the child's facial expression and yet stay far enough away not to inhibit him. A focal length of 80–150mm is ideal (for 35mm format cameras).

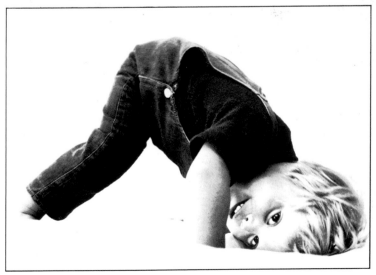

Pick Appropriate Film

The range of films on the market reflects the fact that different types suit different tasks. There are colour films, black-and-white films, and slow, medium and fast films. Which you choose depends on the lighting conditions and the results you want.

● **Use negative film** for snapshots. Colour prints are easy to look at and hand around, and negative film is very forgiving of exposure errors – so it works well in simple cameras. Repeat prints from negatives are cheap.

● **Takes slide for quality.** Colour transparency film gives better definition and finer grain – and does not fade as quickly as negative film. In the home darkroom, it is also easier to print from a slide than from a negative.

● **Use fast film** in dim light or with a fast shutter speed or a small aperture. However, fast film (ISO 800–3200) cannot match the richness of colour and fineness of detail of slow film such as ISO 50 or 100. Medium speed (ISO 200–400) offers a good compromise.

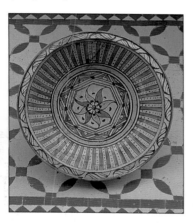

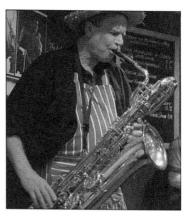

▲ Use a slow film either if the light is bright or when you have complete control over lighting – such as when using flash for the shot above left. In low light, where flash is inappropriate and a slow shutter speed cannot be used – choose a super fast film such as the ISO 1600 variety I used for the jazz musician above.

◄ A slow film (Kodachrome 25) and slight underexposure (1/30, *f*8) produced the rich colours and fine detail of this close-up.

Remember Black and White

Black-and-white film can give scenes a look of gritty realism or graphic beauty. But apart from such aesthetic and stylistic considerations, it is also more flexible than colour film.

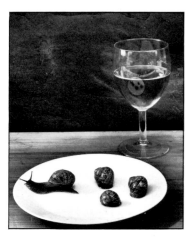

● **Forget filtration** when using black-and-white film indoors. The colour casts that upset colour films in artificial light and daylight are irrelevant with black and white.

● **Process and print** quickly and simply in a home darkroom. Black-and-white processing needs only two or three solutions, and the processing temperatures are low.

● **Increase development** if you are in dim light and need to increase the speed of the film in your camera. To double film speed (eg from ISO 400 to 800) lengthen development by 30 per cent.

● **Control contrast** during development. With flat lighting, extend development time by about 15–20 per cent. Bright sunlight creates high contrast, so cut development by an equal amount. To prevent thin pale negatives when cutting development, overexpose by half a stop.

▲ For overall sharpness and detail choose a fine-grain film.

▼ The long exposure burnt out the highlights, while the grain of the film suggests the dust-laden atmosphere.

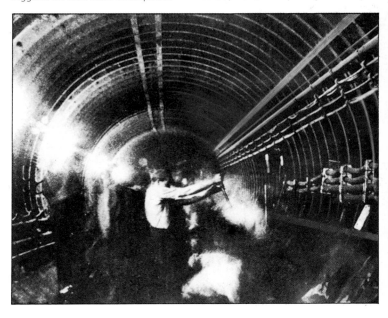

Take a Relaxed Portrait

People are among a photographer's most important subjects. The 24 pages that follow offer suggestions for handling everything from a formal portrait through a celebration such as a wedding to the candid picture snatched on a city street. The first thing to learn is how to get your subject to relax.

● **Eliminate fixed grins** by asking your sitters to breathe in deeply, puff out their cheeks and exhale through pursed lips. This always provokes spontaneous, natural laughter, which you can catch on film.

● **Cure glazed looks** by getting subjects to look down and close their eyes. On the command 'Now!' they look up at the camera, with a fresh and open expression – and you press the shutter release.

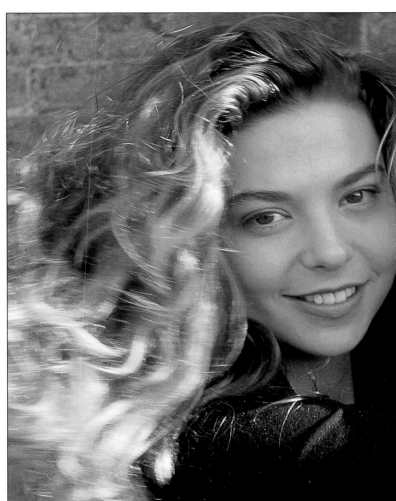

● **Give them something to do.** 'What can I do with my hands?' is the portrait sitter's lament. Most people will adopt a more relaxed pose if they have something to lean against, or perhaps a prop to hold.

● **Shoot a double portrait.** In pairs, people have each other to think about and find it easier to ignore the camera. If you want just one of the pair in the picture, you can space them a few feet apart and crop the print.

● **Use a telephoto lens setting** (in the range 80mm–150mm) so that you can stand a little way off from your subject. Long lenses are more flattering to the subject, too.

▼ I used a telephoto lens setting on a zoom for this informal portrait, choosing the brick wall as a background to complement the young woman's eyes and hair.

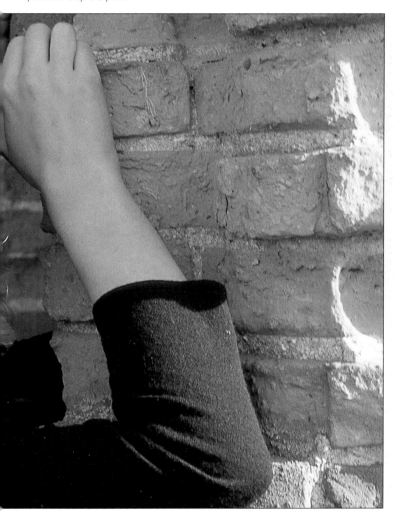

Suggest Character

Traditionally, portrait photographers have tried to flatter by concealing the effects that time has had on the faces of their sitters. By taking the opposite approach – and suggesting visually the subject's experience of life – you can say much more. However, this does not mean photographing people at their worst. Be sympathetic, aim for an honest – but kind – view and you will not only get a better picture, but you will please your subject.

● **Crop in tightly** so that your subject's face fills the frame. By minimizing the surrounding distractions you direct the viewer's eyes to the most important thing: the sitter's face.

● **Use oblique lighting** to reveal the expressive topography of your sitter's features. Soft, non-directional lighting smooths out the wrinkles that make every face unique.

● **Keep a subject talking.** Most people have characteristic gestures that, used in relaxed conversation, help to reveal their personalities.

▼ Cropping tight, with the sun above, has emphasized the wrinkles in the two pictures below – each line on their faces creates its own shadow.

▶ Ebbing light at dusk and a low tide create an appropriate and natural background setting for an old Indonesian fisherwoman.

▼ Strong sidelighting creates a moody portrait, where features are emphasized by dominant shadows.

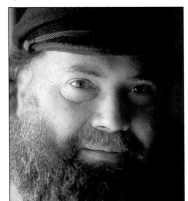

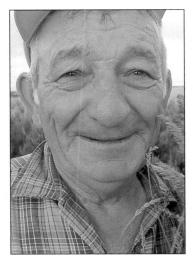

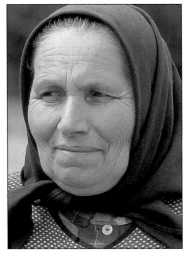

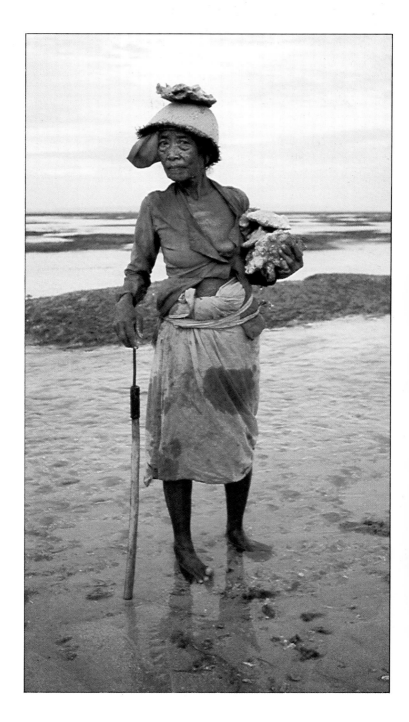

Create a Silhouette

Present an original view of your subject by using backlighting. By controlling exposure carefully, you can create a solid black mass in which the shape is the key to recognition, or opt to reveal just a hint of detail.

● **Choose a background** that is light in tone – a dark background merges with the subject.

● **Pick a bold shape.** Profiles work well in silhouette, but full-face portraits do not.

● **Meter the background** and overexpose by two stops, or …

● **… Meter the subject** and underexpose by two stops.

● **Avoid colour prints** because, unless given special instructions, the processing laboratory will 'compensate' and spoil the silhouette.

● **Boost contrast** by printing black-and-white film on hard paper or by pushing slide film.

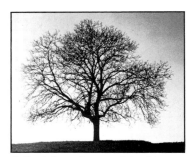

▲ Gradations of tone and detail in silhouettes can range from dramatic outlines with almost no detail, such as the tree above, through high contrast with slight detal (below). The shot of the man required precise exposure, metering from the face, to make sure that his weathered features were recorded on the negative.

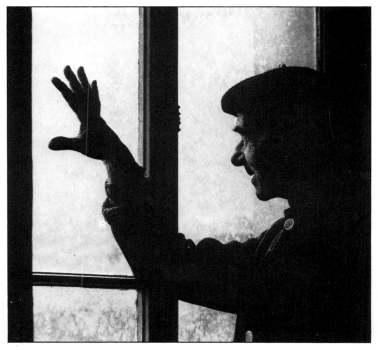

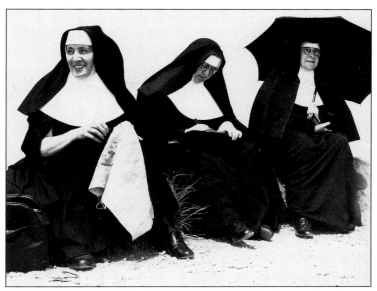

▲ Subjects with inherent high contrast, such as this group of nuns in their black-and-white habits, require careful exposure and printing. I used a high-contrast (Grade 4) printing paper to help to burn out the background.

▼ The silhouette of this castle was achieved simply by metering from the sky – losing all detail from the darker foreground. The pattern of the cloud leaves a strong diagonal in the sky that draws the eye straight to the building.

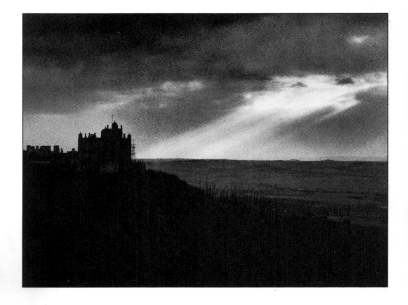

Watch the Background

The background is a living part of any portrait. It can set the scene, play a role, or simply provide an empty stage. A plain backdrop that frees you from distractions enables you to concentrate upon revealing the personality of your subject.

● **Use the stop-down button.**
Unsightly backgrounds, often invisible when focusing an SLR, can be sharper in the final picture. If you have a depth-of-field preview, check the background, and open the aperture if necessary.

● **Light the background** and subject separately in a studio so that you can advance the sitter by adjusting the lights. Achieve separation by making the background one to two stops brighter or darker than the subject.

● **Set a wide aperture** to tidy up a cluttered background. The shallow depth of field that results will hide unsightly details. Take this trick a step further by using a telephoto lens. In bright sunlight and with fast film, use a neutral density filter.

● **Set the scene** by choosing locations that reflect the interests or working environment of the sitter (below right). A wide-angle lens will take in a glimpse of possessions.

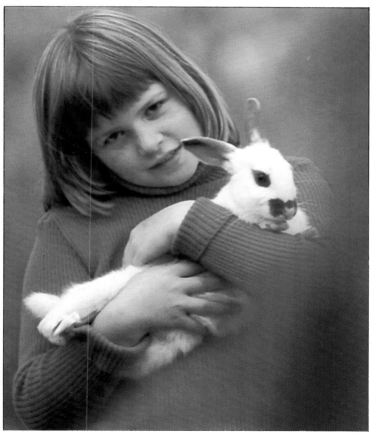

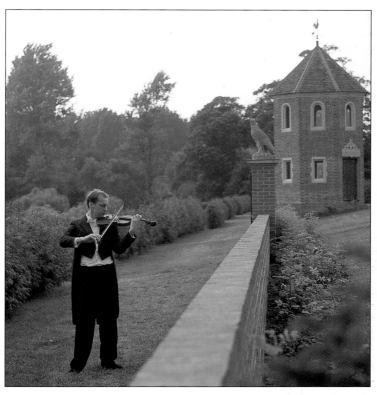

▲ Natural backgrounds (above and left) must be selected with care, otherwise they can detract from the portrait.

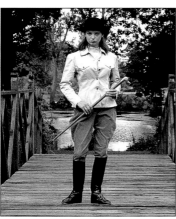

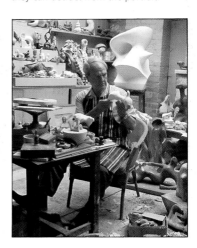

◄ A 400mm lens, at 10m (33ft), blurred the leaves into a green backdrop. The sculptor, Henry Moore was pictured in his studio (right), the cluttered room showing how he worked.

Take a Self-portrait

Taking self-portraits can be demanding, but is also exciting. You get the opportunity to try out techniques and lighting effects to an extent that might demand too much patience from a model.

● **Place a marker** roughly where you intend to stand or sit.

● **Devise** some way of indicating exactly where your head will be. A propped-up cushion will do. Focus and compose on this.

● **Release the shutter** using the camera's self-timer, a long cable (or air) release, or the remote release of a motor-driven camera. If your hand appears in the picture, press an air release with your foot.

● **Use a mirror** to photograph your reflection. This is easier if you are using a waist-level finder than it is with an eye-level finder. You must remember to reverse the negative when you make the print.

● **Experiment.** Try fitting a wide-angle lens and pointing the camera at your face from arm's length.

▼ I used a long air release to take this picture of myself in the studio.

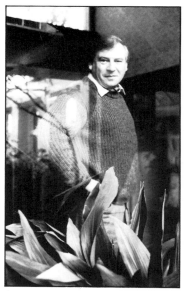

▲ I took this self-portrait by mounting the camera on a tripod outside the window, setting the self-timer, and then moving quickly inside to adopt the pose.

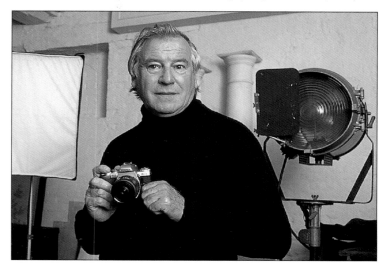

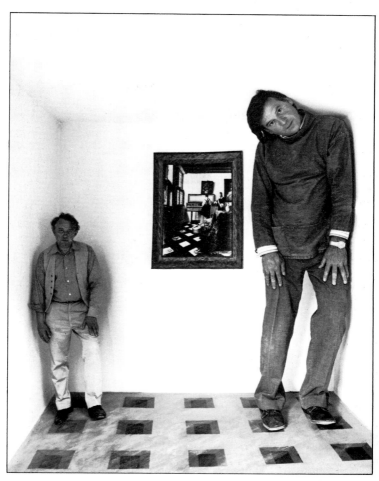

▲ This self-portrait called for a special prop, known as an Ames room after the painter who devised it. Of course, both of us are of normal height – it is the room that is abnormal. The original idea of the room was to show how memory conditions us to jump to conclusions – in this instance that the room is rectangular with its walls and floor at right angles. In fact, it is distorted: the rear wall is almost 4.2 m (14 ft) high and the point where I am standing only about 1.5 m (5 ft) high. From one particular point – at which I set up my camera – the perspective appears normal.

Soften the Mood

The camera records what its lens sees – which is not necessarily what the eye sees. As a result, halcyon days and romantic summer afternoons are sometimes less idyllic on film than they are in memory. To recapture the mood, nature may have to be helped.

● **Add soft focus,** either with a soft-focus filter or with a home-made substitute. Try smearing petroleum jelly onto the skylight filter (not onto the lens itself) or stretching a piece of clear plastic over a lens hood.

● **Use black-and-white film.** Black-and-white images of people and places suggest the days before colour film was widely used, days when family snapshots faded in dog-eared albums.

● **Tint the image sepia.** With colour film, fit a sepia filter – a Wratten 81EF is a good choice. Black-and-white prints, even those that are produced by commercial laboratories, can be toned, in daylight, with kits sold by specialist photographic shops.

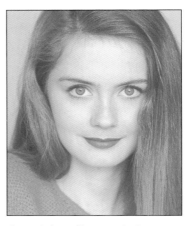

▲ A soft-focus filter over the lens creates a dreamy-looking portrait.

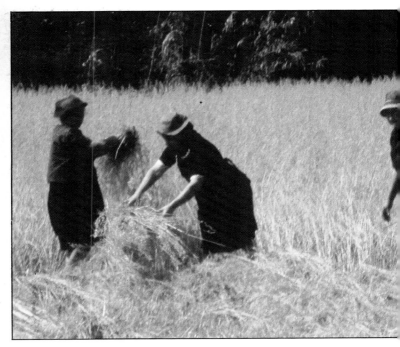

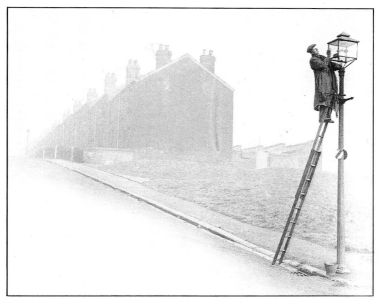

▼ Fast film, underexposure and soft focus put this harvest back 100 years.

▲ Sepia aged a scene already made old-fashioned by high-key and vignetting.

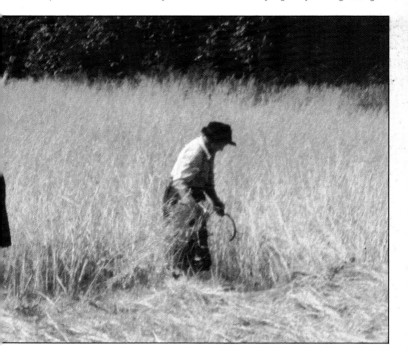

Capture Group Identity

Large groups of people can be difficult to photograph – if you take too casual an approach to your subjects, there is a danger that your picture will show them as individuals and that the feature that unifies everyone will not be clear. Careful grouping and a well-chosen location can help you to avoid this.

● **Use chairs and stairs** to elevate some members of the group above the rest: if everyone's head is at the same height, the composition will lack variety and interest.

● **Sit some of them down.** This too will add variety and interest to the shape of the group.

● **Take lots of pictures.** The more people in a group, the greater the chance that someone's eyes will be closed when the shutter is open. Extra pictures are an insurance policy.

● **Move people together.** The camera makes people appear farther apart than they were. To create unity and form, position them tightly together.

● **Make them work.** When everyone pulls together (as in the picture below) their common interest is obvious.

● **Respect hierarchy.** Most groups have a leader and a formal structure. If it exists, your picture will be stronger for emphasizing it.

● **Get their attention** by blowing a whistle or making a startling noise just before taking the photograph. In big groups everyone talks and looks away from the camera until a trick like this makes them stare at it.

● **Be prepared** to take candid pictures as the group breaks up. Informal groups, such as departing wedding guests often express the spirit of the occasion best.

▼ Arranging a group portrait with people at different distances from the camera can create a dynamic composition where the viewer's eye is encouraged to move from face to face.

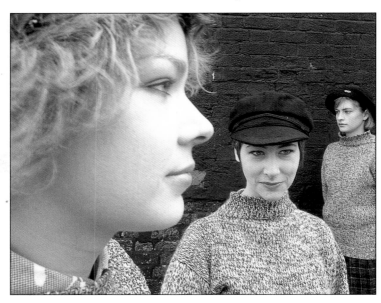

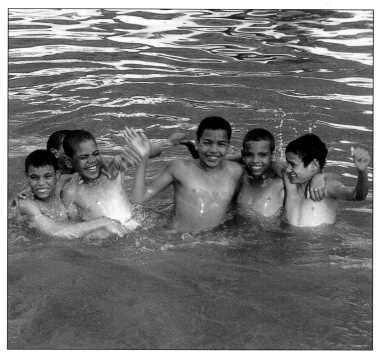

▲ For this informal shot, relaxed expressions and water spray are more crucial than the actual arrangement of the boys in the frame.

▼ The members of a brass band arranged themselves into a visually appealing group with no prompting from the photographer.

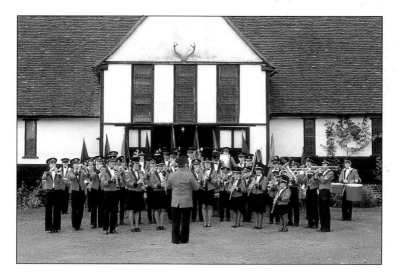

Catch the Good Times

If you can keep your head while all around you are losing theirs … you are not having a good time. But unless you do, party pictures are likely to display the rawest of faults: out-of-focus blur, decapitated trunks, sloping verticals. Be aware of the problems, however, and you plan to avoid them.

● **Consider using a 35mm** snapshot camera. These do everything – including focusing – for you, leaving you free to talk to your friends and enjoy yourself.

● **Use a wide-angle lens** on an SLR. It will reduce the need for accurate focusing and will let you get a reasonably broad view, even at a crowded party.

● **Do not forget** the formal views. At weddings and similar functions there are some pictures that simply must be taken – such as the bride and groom on the church steps. If you are the only photographer at the wedding, and you miss these, you are unlikely to be invited to the christening!

● **Watch** for 'grab shots'. People let their hair down at celebrations. For tips on this, see pages 40–41.

● **Use an auto flash.** Juggling guide numbers slows you down: with auto flash and program exposure you need never change aperture or shutter speed. Autofocus SLRs and flash-guns have infrared emitters which take the strain out of focusing in the dark.

● **Change flash batteries** before you start taking pictures or you will be forever waiting for the ready light to come on.

● **Move close** in smoky rooms. Smoke cuts contrast, dilutes colours and reflects light from a flash.

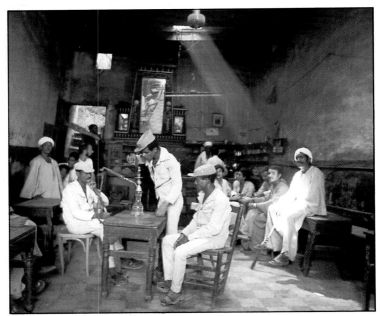

▲ Preparations for a convivial gathering in an Egyptian café are caught by a wide-angle lens, which even at an aperture of *f*3.5 gives good depth of field (and covers the whole room). The shaft of sunlight illustrates how smoke can obscure detail in a picture taken in close conditions.

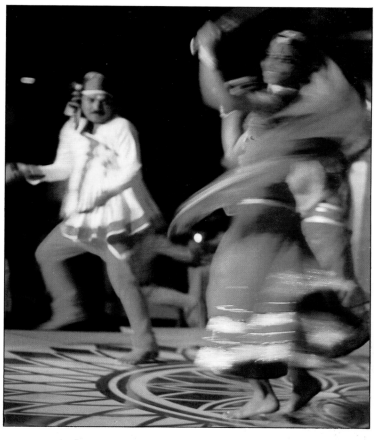

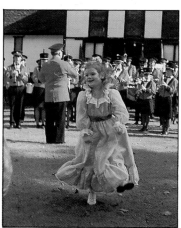

▲ I wanted movement in the picture of dancers, so shot at 1/15, but used 1/250 to catch the bridesmaid (left) celebrating after a wedding. The same wedding produced the informal shot below of a formal occasion – reading the telegrams.

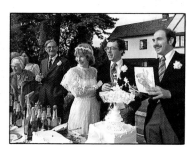

Record the Zest of Youth

Children are marvellous subjects – spontaneous, energetic, uninhibited and expressive. They are best photographed when they are engrossed in some activity, but a record of their progress from birth to adolescence should include a few more formal portraits taken at important milestones.

● **Vary the angle of view.** For natural portraits, lower the camera to the child's eye-level, by kneeling or lying on the floor. However, shots taken from above or below can also work.

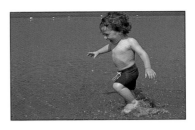

● **Give children time** to forget your presence. They have short attention spans and will soon lose any self-consciousness. A telephoto lens will get you away from the immediate vicinity.

● **Use a wide aperture** and a fast shutter speed when you want to freeze rapid movement and soften the background, and …

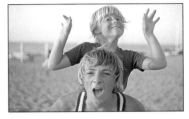

● **… Use a small aperture** and a slow shutter speed when you want to show movement through a blur against a sharp background.

● **Pre-set the camera** and load fast film when you are uncertain what will happen next.

● **Photograph babies** in warm, calm and familiar surroundings with the mother close at hand.

▼ Letting children get on with what they are doing, whether playing (top) or eating (below), means that you can concentrate on getting a good picture without having to hold the subject's attention. Even if kids play up to the camera (above), this behaviour in itself can make an amusing picture.

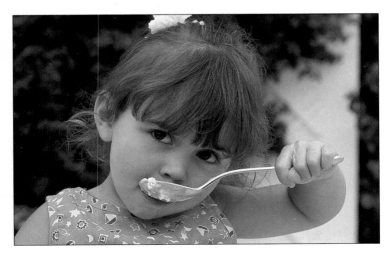

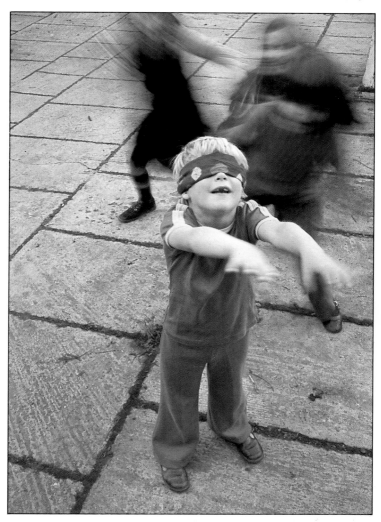

▲ I braced myself against a wall to take the game of blindman's bluff at 1/15 and an aperture of f16, using a 35mm lens to cover the whirling figures. The shot of the smiling boy (right) required a wide aperture of f2.8 to ensure that the background became blurred.

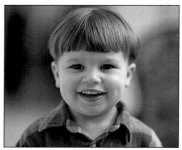

Abstract the Nude

To gain the experience needed to cope with the formidable difficulties of photographing the human body, begin with the abstract. Lessons learned about form, tone and texture will stand you in good stead when you come to advanced full figure work.

● **Choose the light** that best creates the mood you are seeking. Sidelighting divides the body into dramatic areas of light and shade, and emphasizes form.

● **Frame tightly** to focus attention on just one area of the body.

● **Avoid depicting** the face, which, by suggesting personality and character, leads away from the abstract.

● **Stop down** to increase depth of field. Unsharp areas are distracting in tightly framed photographs.

● **Emphasize skin texture** with baby oil or cold water.

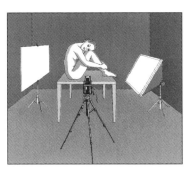

▲ To emphasize form in this abstract shot, a single light was placed to the side of the nude, with a reflector opposite to avoid excessive shadows.

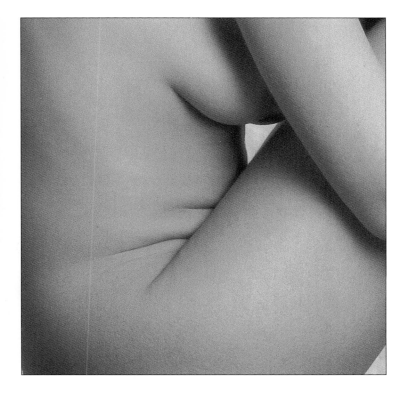

Reveal the World of Work

The fascination of other people's jobs gives portraits taken in a working environment an extra element that is lacking in the studio. Pose the person near the camera, but include background details that identify the job.

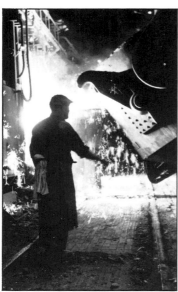

● **Use a wide-angle lens** and stand farther back than you would for a portrait – the background will explain what kind of work is being done.

● **Capture activity.** A portrait of someone working looks better than a static shot of them with the tools of their trade. Of course, if they are concentrating on their work, they will be less conscious of the camera.

● **Seek a viewpoint** that is unusual. The face of the steelworker on the left is completely hidden, yet the harsh blaze of light behind him clearly expresses the harshness of his working conditions – and hints at the toughness of his character.

▲ Available light alone was needed to capture the dramatic work of a foundry. A sea of sheep, below, clearly places the rider in his working context.

● **Take fast film** and flash. The lighting available in industrial locations is often totally inadequate for photography. You may not only have to use fast film, but you may have to uprate its speed as well. A small portable flash is often useful for lighting figures that are close to the camera.

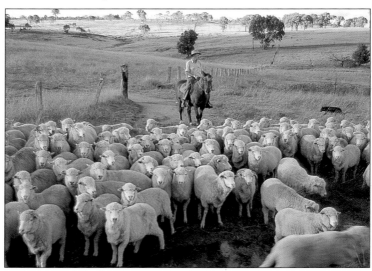

Catch People Unawares

By using the techniques of photojournalism not only can you take street scenes that are humorous, intimate or even newsworthy, but also acquire the skills that will make it easy to create candid, relaxed pictures of your family and your friends.

● **Pre-focus the camera** and select a small aperture – a 50mm lens setting focused at 2m (7ft) and stopped down to *f*16 will render everything from about 1.3m (4ft) to 7m (21ft) acceptably sharp. You can 'point and shoot' without having to focus.

● **Use a wide-angle lens** for pictures like that on the right in which you need both depth of field and coverage.

● **Load fast negative film** which allows you to set a small aperture and a fast shutter speed and tolerates exposure errors.

● **Move in close.** Many pictures are spoiled because the main subject is a tiny shape in the middle of the frame.

● **Be decisive.** When you see the picture you want, sight, shoot, and lower the camera again. The subject may not even notice.

● **Do not be content** with one picture. If your subject seems willing to be photographed again, improve the composition and take further shots.

● **Teach yourself** to shoot from the hip. A camera held at waist-level is far less noticeable than one raised to eye-level.

● **Be prepared.** Unless the camera is in your hand, ready, you will miss all the best pictures.

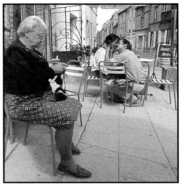

▲ Human interest adds colour. An informal picture of a loving couple, ignored by an elderly woman, captures the flavour of France; below, holiday hats link a mother and her children intent on quenching their thirst.

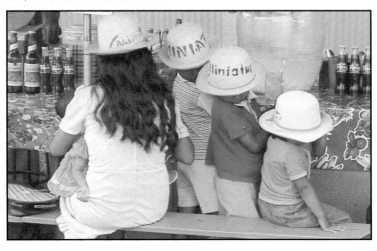

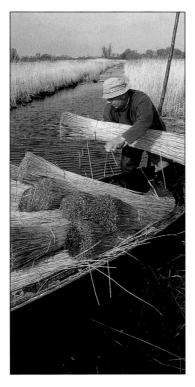

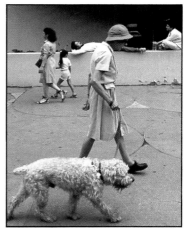

▲ New York's Guggenheim Museum provides a backdrop for a relaxed picture of city dwellers.

◀ Careful composition clearly shows the art of reed-cutting against the backdrop of the Norfolk Broads.

▼ This portrait of people working in a paddy field shows their hard work framed in the geometry of the field.

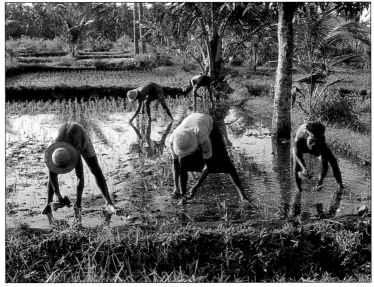

Make Photos Tell a Story

Every picture tells a story, but a single picture lacks an essential element in story-telling: what happened next? A picture sequence enables you to portray a dynamic situation from start to finish, to show triumph and disaster, and to record what was going on around the main subject as the thread of the story developed.

● **Plan ahead.** If you know where the action is likely to take place – as I did when shooting the sports day shown here – you can pick the best viewpoints well in advance.

● **Vary the scale,** by moving closer to, or farther away from, the subject or by using lenses of different focal lengths.

▼ Telling the story of a sports day involves several chapters. To portray a race you need several pictures of the action – one or more that tell the result, such as the bottom shot of the boy who came in last.

● **Turn the camera** so that not all your pictures are horizontal.

● **Cheat!** If you miss a particularly good moment that you need for your story, ask the participants to repeat it for you.

● **Spectators** are often as interesting as what they are watching and their expressions – like those of the schoolboys below – can offer clues to what is happening behind the camera.

● **Plan the presentation** carefully. Vary the print size and make sure that you use a well-composed layout.

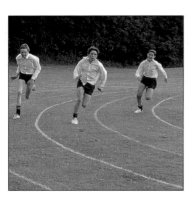

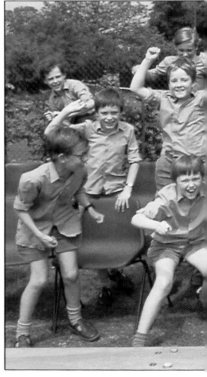

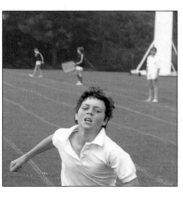

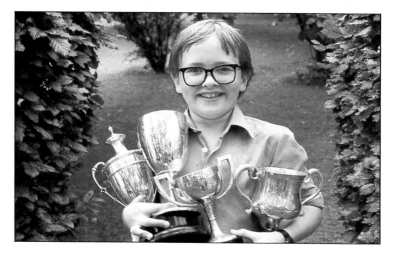

▲ A jubilant smile and an armful of trophies say everything about a possible future champion's day of glory.

▼ Whatever is going on behind the camera, crowd reaction provides a living link in the picture sequence.

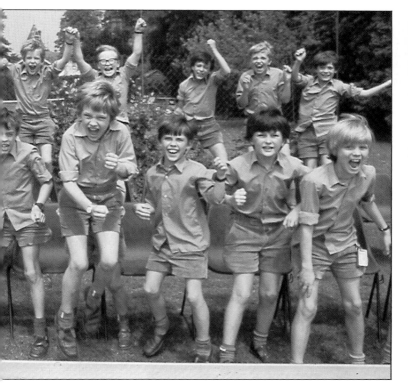

Make Shadows Work

Photography is painting with light. The next 20 pages are devoted to light in all its forms, from daylight to stroboscopic light. The section begins by examining the opposite of light – shadow.

● **Use glancing light** early or late in the day to reveal shadows not at their strongest, but at their longest.

● **Watch out** for your own shadow, which may creep into the picture if the sun is behind you.

● **Use hard lighting** to make shadows as bold as possible. Outdoors, bright sunlight casts deep shadows. Indoors, use a naked bulb or a small flash unit.

● **Control exposure** carefully. Take meter readings from the brightly lit areas so that shadows look dark and mysterious.

● **Use slide film** for best colour results. Negative film has more latitude and retains detail, weakening the impact.

▼ Shadows can make subjects in their own right – here acting as a counterpoint to the object that created them.

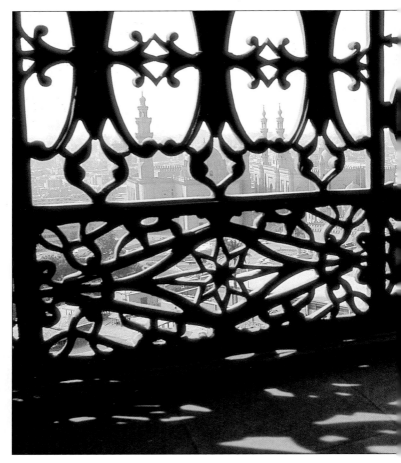

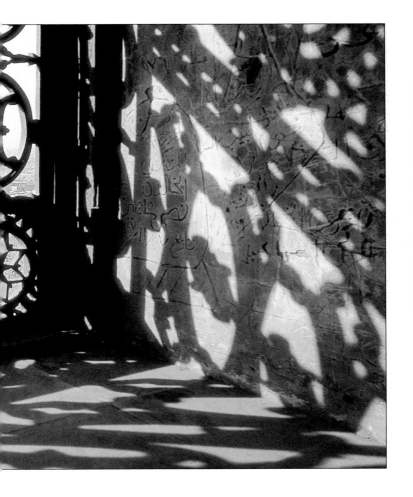

Pick your Sunlight

A studio is a place where the direction of lighting can be controlled. Similar control can be achieved outdoors if you choose the right time of day or vary your viewpoint.

● **Use frontal lighting,** with the sun behind you, to maximize colour. Colours are at their most brilliant when they are reflecting the sun.

● **Use sidelighting** to accentuate the texture and form of a subject. With sidelighting, subjects become a mixture of shadow and highlight – exaggerating their three-dimensionality. This works for simple subjects, but can look confusing if there is a mass of shapes.

● **Minimize mist and haze** by standing with the sun to one side. Cross-lighting picks out distinct features more efficiently than overhead light or direct frontal light.

● **Add atmosphere** by shooting into the sun. This washes out colours and creates a dynamic picture – particularly when the sun appears in the photograph. Make sure, though, that the lens is clean because dust and fingerprints will create flare.

● **Make bold shapes** by placing your subject between the sun and the camera. This creates a silhouette with a brilliant halo around it.

● **Suggest heat** by taking pictures at noon – small shadows directly beneath your subjects vividly conjure up the feeling of a hot day.

▼ Patience, determination and perception produce good photographs – and when you are trying for trick shots like the one below, in which the sun looks as if it has just rolled down the side of the pyramid, that means great accuracy in camera angles, focusing and judgment of exposure. I took the picture at dawn, having determined exactly where the sun would rise, and gave an exposure of 1/250 at *f*11 on ISO 64 film. In a photograph like this colours are deliberately muted, and the elements allowed to become silhouettes, in order to emphasize the composition.

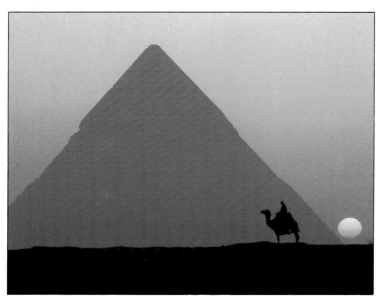

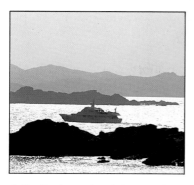

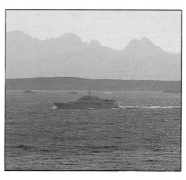

▲ The first in a series of pictures taken over 15 minutes shows the subject backlit by a high sun. A 200mm lens pulls the mountains up, but both they and the yacht are almost totally in shadow. In the next shot, taken as the boat moves away from the sun's path, light creeps round its stern. All shots were exposed for the highlights.

▼ The sun strikes the yacht from the rear in the third shot, modelling its detail. Flag colours and a brown tender can be seen. At this angle the reflected wake gives a strong sense of momentum and the background is sharper. As the yacht moves into sunlight in the fourth picture, it reflects the blue sea.

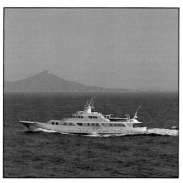

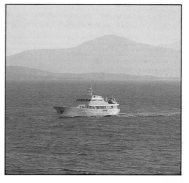

► Finally, the yacht has rounded the headland completely and has moved into full sun. Direct frontal light has made the sea a brilliant blue, but the yacht looks flat. The tender can now be seen to be red, not brown.

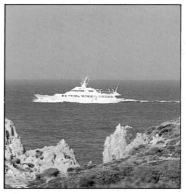

Use Light to Reveal Form

The camera turns three-dimensional reality into a two-dimensional print or slide – it cannot reproduce solidity and depth, but it can suggest them effectively if the subject is properly lit. The key is to avoid direct frontal light.

● **Use sidelighting,** which will create shadows that in turn will create the modelling that is needed to suggest the model's form.

● **Soften the artificial lighting** either by bouncing it from a white surface, even something as simple as newspaper, or by diffusing it with a sheet of tracing paper or cloth.

● **Turn the subject** so that its most characteristic surface faces the camera.

● **Soften the shadows** by using reflectors or fill-in lamps.

▼ Patterns of light and shade, cast by sunlight shining through a window, are a key factor in lending a sense of roundness and depth to the figure.

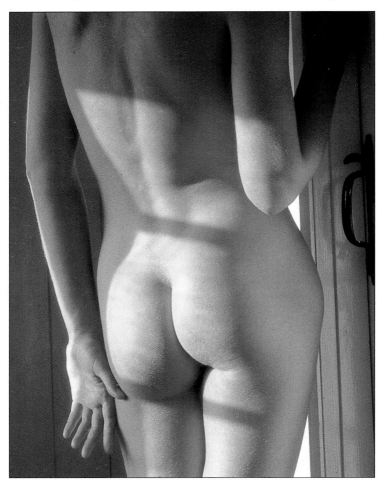

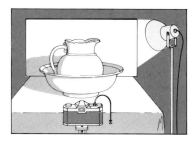

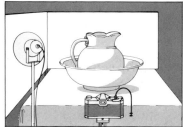

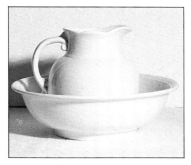

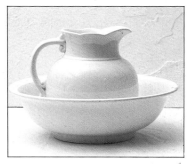

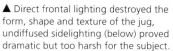

▲ Direct frontal lighting destroyed the form, shape and texture of the jug, undiffused sidelighting (below) proved dramatic but too harsh for the subject.

▲ The best result was obtained when light was bounced off a side screen onto both the jug and the background, softening shadows and creating good modelling.

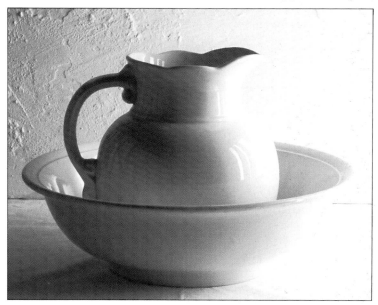

Reflect the Light

Strong directional lighting throws deep shadows that can obscure subtle detail. A simple reflector will lighten the shadows and reduce the contrast, creating a more delicate, softer image.

● **Make reflectors from** any white or shiny surface. The reflector should be bigger than the subject.

● **Use foil or silver card** for directional fill-in light. Crumpled foil scatters light.

● **Use mirrors** for the most brilliant reflection of all.

● **Position a reflector** opposite the main light source.

● **Curve the reflector inwards** to concentrate the light.

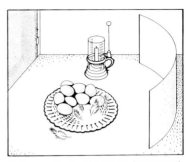

▼ A curved reflector lent such tone and texture to these eggs that they seem three-dimensional in the photograph.

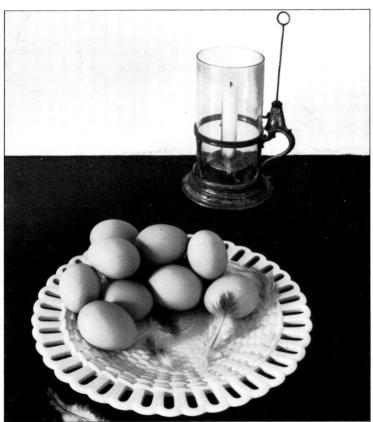

Correct Colour

When precise colour fidelity is of paramount importance, use correction filters to balance the light falling on the subject to match the correct temperature of the film.

● **Use 81 series filters** in overcast weather. These pale yellow filters range from 81 (almost colourless) to an 81EF, which is tobacco-coloured. They remove the blue cast from pictures taken in cloudy weather and, in sunny conditions, correct the colour of shaded subjects lit only by blue sky.

● **Use 82 series filters** in the reddish light of dusk, 62, 82A, 82B and 82C filters are pale blue, so they prevent scenes lit by late afternoon sunlight looking too warm in hue.

● **Use two filters** – an 80A and an 82B – when taking pictures in domestic light with daylight-balanced film. If you have tungsten-balanced film in the camera, use an 82B only.

● **Shoot colour negative** film if you do not want to bother with filtration. All but the heaviest of colour casts can be correct during printing.

● **Remember** that you can deliberately use colour casts to create unusual effects in colour pictures.

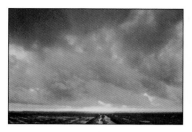

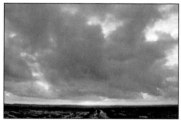

▲ Orange filters are usually used to correct coloration when using tungsten-balanced slide film in daylight. Here, however, one has been used to turn an unfiltered sunset to a golden landscape.

▼ An 81C yellow filter counteracts a blue cast from an overcast sky.

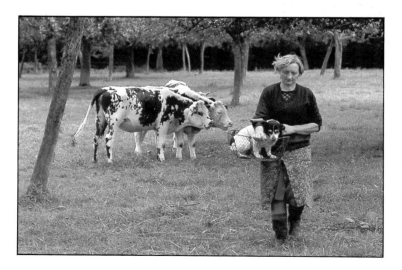

Create Atmosphere

Transparent and translucent subjects are at their most attractive when lit from behind. If the subject is also coloured, backlighting makes hues seem richer and colours more saturated. The technique calls for careful judgement of exposure.

● **Measure exposure** by moving in close to the subject. If you do not, the effect of the backlighting will cause you to underexpose.

● **Create contrast** by including both translucent and opaque objects in the picture. In contrast to the clear objects, the opaque will appear as silhouettes.

● **Add light** if you want to retain detail in non-transparent objects. Use a small flash-gun (see page 60) or a reflector close to the camera.

● **Use filters** if the subject has no colour. A deep red filter, for example may add interest to a backlit subject.

▶ The Buddhist monk was taken on ISO 50 film with an exposure of 1/250 at *f*8. Backlit palm leaves show densities of hues (below) that would not have been revealed by reflected light.

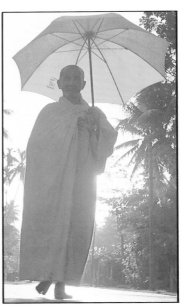

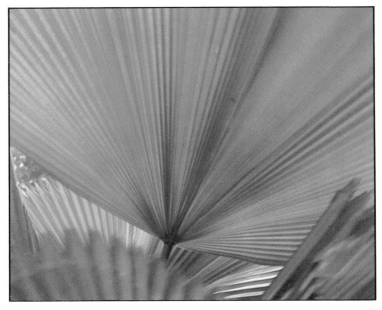

Pick your Moment

The colour of natural light changes during the course of the day, varying from the deepest red through white to brilliant blue. By scheduling your photography with this is mind, you can choose the type and direction of light that suits your subject best.

● **Get up early** to catch the day at its best. Early morning light has an exquisite clarity that is never quite matched later in the day.

● **Shoot at dusk** or dawn to capture the warm sunlight, rich in atmosphere. At the end of the day, when there is still some light in the sky, the street and house lights can add a colourful contrast.

● **Avoid midday.** When the sun is overhead, it casts harsh, unflattering shadows straight downwards. This is the worst light for revealing form.

● **Use long lenses early.** Focal lengths longer than 200mm emphasize haze and other atmospheric effects and give best results just after the sun has risen, when the air is cool and clear.

● **Make it quick** at sunrise and sunset. At these times of day, the light changes minute by minute.

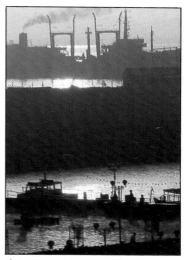

▲ A 200mm lens caught Bombay at sunset. Below, frost, preserved by a gate's bars, gave substance to shadows.

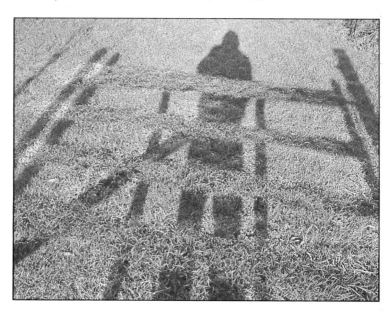

Light for Contrast

Hard lighting produces high contrast between the shadows and the highlights of a picture. Use it when you want to create a sense of drama by infusing your pictures with mystery and menace.

● **Use one small light** such as a bare light bulb or a small portable flash to the side of the subject.

● **The closer the light** is to the subject, the greater the contrast will be.

● **Base exposure** on the highlights to ensure that the shadow areas fill in and create solid black shapes.

● **Block off other lights.**

▶ A diffused flash to the side of the camera creates contours of light and dark across the model's face. Available light from the window produced the contrast in the picture below.

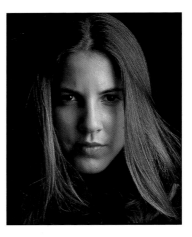

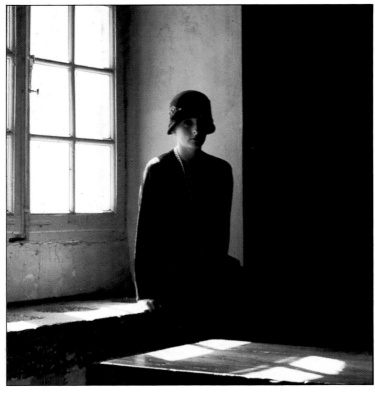

Light for Detail

Soft directional lighting flatters a subject, reveals detail even in shadow and adds warmth and modelling to surfaces. Use it when character is important.

● **Use large light sources** such as natural window light or light from an overcast sky.

● **Diffuse the light** of small sources by placing tracing paper or white fabric in front of the reflector, bulb, flash or window.

● **Reflect light** from a white wall or ceiling. This has the effect of softening and spreading the beam.

● **Fill in the shadows** by adding extra lights near the camera. Make sure, though, that the multiple light sources do not create multiple shadows.

● **Use reflectors** to fill in shadows (as explained on page 51).

▶ Photofloods were bounced off the ceiling to soften the light and eliminate the hard shadows.

▼ A casserole was placed on a check cloth chosen for its tone, and lit by a window light and a reflector.

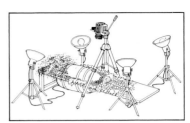

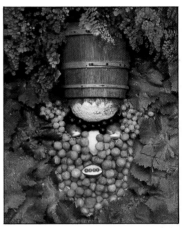

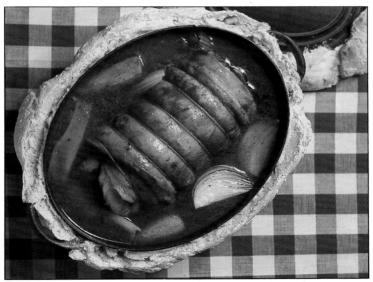

Reveal Texture

Even heavily textured materials can look flat and dull unless you take steps to bring out the lines and furrows that criss-cross their surfaces. Raking light – oblique directional light – is the key to creating texture, but take care with colour film to soften deep shadows or detail will be lost. Landscapes aside, texture is best revealed by moving in close to the subject.

● **Search for texture.** Water, wind and frost etch surfaces in different ways.

● **Choose directional light.** Flat, diffuse lighting conceals texture.

● **Control colour contrast.** To reveal texture, colour film demands softer lighting than black-and-white film does. Use reflectors or fill-in flash if raking light is very bright.

▶ Architectural detail is revealed by light at an angle of 40° and, at *f*22, underexposed by half a stop.

▼ Three hours later than the first picture was taken, slanting evening sunlight brought out the ruggedness of the Norwegian landscape.

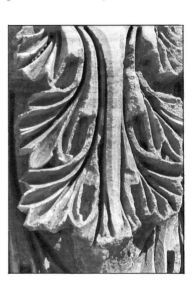

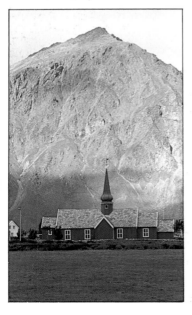

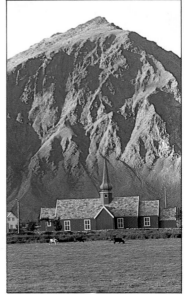

Catch the Gleam of Glass

Glass and liquids, although transparent, always have shape: modelling or reflections will always produce an image on film. There are problems associated with photographing glass – but they do have solutions.

● **Use backlighting** to reveal transparency fully.

● **Add colour** to clear glass by filling with coloured liquid.

● **Use reflections** to define the edges of glassware. If a bottle merges with a white background, place black cards on either side of it, just outside the picture. This creates black lines on either side of the bottle.

● **Add bubbles** to liquid by blowing through a straw or by using a syringe.

● **Cope with melting ice** by substituting plastic ice cubes, obtainable from movie prop shops.

● **Use backgrounds** to show the shape of glass. Normal or recognizable backgrounds are best.

▼ A collection of glass containers makes a fascinating composition, as the transparency of the glass varies as the lighting is changed. Use a neutral background so that colours and shadows stand out well.

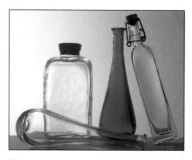

▼ Campari on ice called for a careful balance of lighting and background. The glass was lit from below through a hole cut in black card placed on a lightbox.

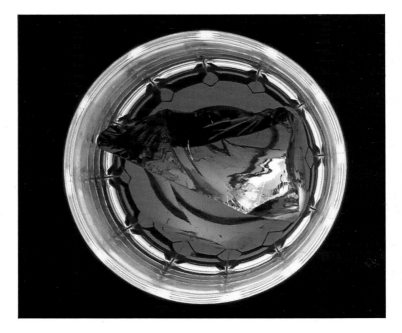

Freeze with Flash

All but a handful of SLR cameras have top shutter speeds of 1/2000 or greater, yet this brief exposure may not be quite short enough to arrest the movement of the fastest moving subject. To stop such rapid action, you should rely not upon the shutter but upon your electronic flash-gun.

● **Use an auto flash,** not a manual gun. Manual flash units emit a pulse of light of fixed duration, whereas an automatic gun produces a variable and usually much shorter pulse, which can last for as little as 1/40,000 of a second.

● **Set the shutter** to the fastest speed that will synchronize with flash, to avoid a 'ghost' image appearing on the film.

● **Choose a wide aperture.** If your flash offers a choice of apertures, select the widest (a low *f* number) to ensure that the flash is as short as possible.

● **Move close** to your subject. At near-subject distances the flash unit cuts off the pulse of light most rapidly.

● **Bracket your pictures,** because the auto-exposure facility on the flash unit may not be completely reliable when the subject is very close.

● **Take lots of pictures,** because an element of luck is involved in this technique. The more pictures you take, the greater your chances of success and the greater the number of variations you will capture.

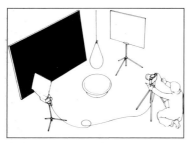

▶ Portable flash giving an exposure time of about 1/1000 was used to freeze the bursting balloon. The flash-gun was to one side, angled at 45°, and facing a large silverized mirror. A slight delay was needed between firing the air pistol and releasing the shutter. A second balloon was used for the third picture.

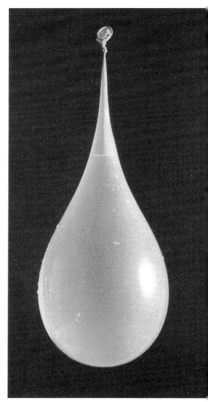

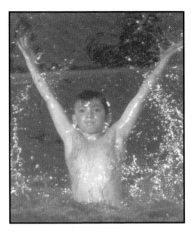

▲ A single portable flash cut out an unwanted background and froze the spray into individual drops.

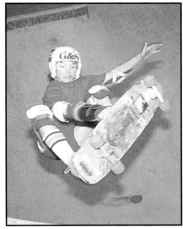

▲ Poor light called for a shutter speed of 1/60 – flash stopped the action with good detail.

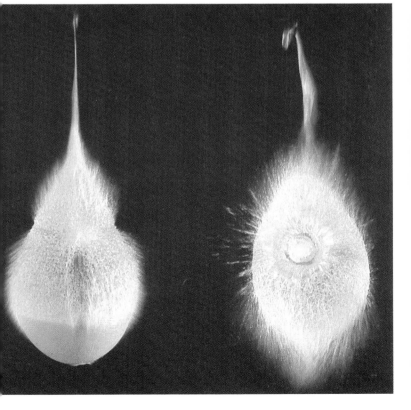

Mix Flash and Daylight

Natural light can produce extreme contrast between highlight and shadow – midday sun, for example, leaves deep pools of darkness in the eye sockets and under the chin. By using electronic flash in daylight as a fill-in light you can reduce contrast and create an image with richer, brighter colours.

● **Reduce contrast** by using a flash for backlit subjects.

● **Increase contrast** by using flash on a dull day. This will help your subject to stand out from a dull background, and will increase colour saturation.

● **Many SLRs now have flash-guns** built in. These are ideal for fill-in flash, and can do the necessary exposure calculations for you. Many hot-shoe fitted guns can also be used for automatic fill-in.

● **With older flash-guns** and cameras, balance exposure for the background and the area lit by flash. Set the dial on the flash unit to double the film's ISO rating, pick an aperture from the options and check the exposure meter to see if the shutter speed is slow enough for flash: if not, choose a smaller aperture.

● **Fill-in flash** works over short distances: you should be between 1.3–3m (4–10ft) from your subject.

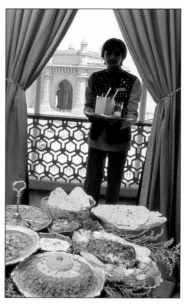

▲ In the picture above flash has been used to decrease the overall contrast in the scene. With the window being far brighter than the exotic food in the foreground, the extra illumination has helped to restore reasonable detail to all areas of the scene.

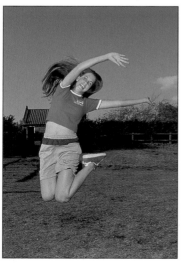

◀ Fill-in flash was used in the picture of a girl jumping to ensure that she stood out well against the background. The flash rather than a fast shutter speed was responsible for freezing her movement, as the burst of light only lasts from 1/2000–1/40,000.

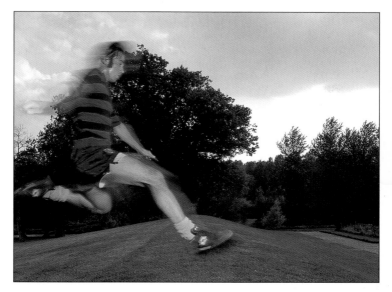

▲ Using a slower than usual shutter speed along with fill-in flash to capture a moving subject close to the camera creates a double exposure – a blurred image of the runner at 1/30 is instantly sandwiched with a pin-sharp one caught by the brief burst of flash.

▼ The intense light thrown by the welding torch threw everything around it into heavy shadow, unrelieved by the weak daylight from a nearby window. An exposure measured from the torch gave a highlight reading of *f*16, while the reading from daylight on the figure was *f*2.8. After calculating an aperture of *f*8 for flash, I allowed two extra stops for the daylight and the torch (setting the aperture at *f*16) and shot at a speed of 1/15 to record the spark trails. Slight movement then effectively softened the image.

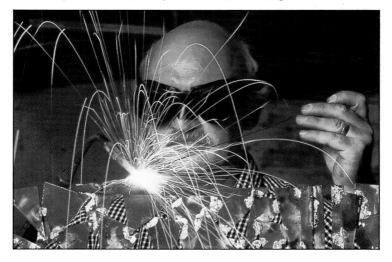

Bounce Flash Accurately

The simplest way to use electronic flash is to lock the unit firmly into the camera's hot-shoe and point the flash at the subject. But this snapshot approach yields flat lighting and unattractive, hard-edged shadows. Bouncing the flash from a ceiling or a wall produces far better results.

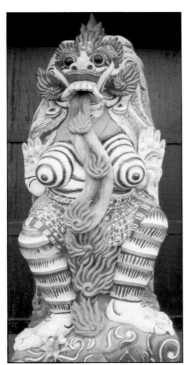

▼ Although this interior scene is predominantly lit by diffuse sunlight from a window, the ambient light alone would have created far harsher shadows. Bouncing light from a flash unit off the ceiling helps to soften the harsh contrast.

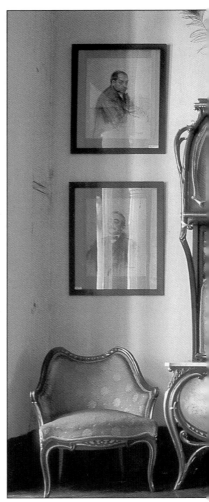

▲ Pattern has a habit of seeming to flatten an object, particularly if the picture is taken in soft, shadowless light. To bring out the bright colours and the violent patterns of the fire-breathing Balinese demon, I used a flash-gun positioned close to the camera. I diffused its light by bouncing it off a reflector. The intention of the lighting was to bring the statue nearer to the abstract so that the viewer would forget what it was and think of it simply as pattern – a decorative feature. Perfect symmetry and flat lighting tend to strengthen pattern.

● **Use a tilt-head flash,** which has a head that can point upwards. Most modern SLR cameras can meter flash output through the lens, so that the amount of flash required can still be calculated automatically.

● **Find a white surface.** Coloured surfaces absorb or tint reflected light.

● **If you have to calculate exposure** for an older gun or camera, you must calculate the total distance from flash to subject via the reflecting surface. You should then double this, to allow for the fact that walls are less-than-perfect reflectors. Use this distance to calculate the aperture and/or flash mode needed.

● **Stay relatively close** to your subject to make the best use of the broadly based flash beam.

● **Carry extra batteries** because the flash unit operates at full power for every picture and cells soon run down.

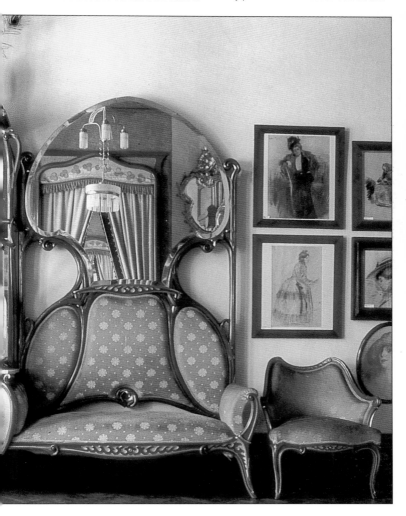

Mix Natural and Tungsten

Colour casts, created by using a colour film wrongly balanced for the light source (for example, daylight film in tungsten light), are usually to be avoided. But what do you do when the light falling on the subject is mixed? Follow a few simple rules and you can use such conditions to create pictures of striking beauty.

● **Let one light source** dominate. If different sources illuminate equal areas, the picture will look confusing.

● **Pick film carefully.** Films balanced for daylight or tungsten light will give accurate colour when they are used appropriately. Use daylight film with a tungsten source and you will get an orange cast; use tungsten film in daylight and you will get a blue cast. Accuracy is not always important: by deliberately breaking the rules and photographing Dylan Thomas's house, below, with tungsten film, I created purple tints that made the estuary look exciting in rather dull light.

● **Use light-balancing filters.** The light-balancing filters – the yellowish series 81 and the bluish series 82 – can be used in various strengths to exaggerate or to reduce colour casts. An 80A filter turns daylight-balanced film into tungsten-balanced and an 85 filter converts tungsten film to daylight.

● **Shoot negative film** and adjust colour in the darkroom. Negative film has great tolerance for light of the 'wrong' colour. If you do not like the first print from a negative made in mixed light, you can alter the colours by changing the enlarger filter pack. Fast negative films are most tolerant.

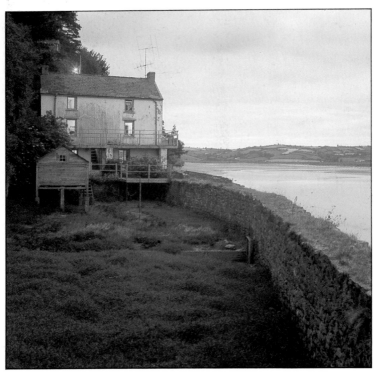

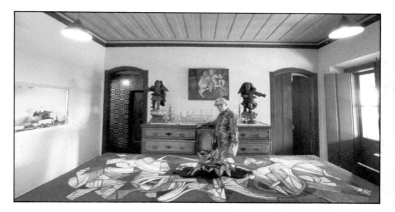

◀ Dylan Thomas's house was photographed at sunset on tungsten film. A mixture of daylight, tungsten lights and bounced flash was used to light the room above: daylight film has given the ceiling lights an orange glow.

▶ For the picture of the hotel forecourt either daylight or tungsten film could have been used: I chose tungsten film to bring up the blues.

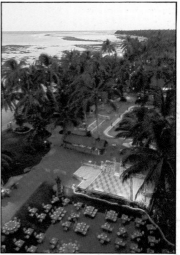

▼ The Ritz Hotel dining room has been captured by using daylight film and carefully balancing daylight and artificial light. The daylight film has warmed the light from the tungsten bulbs in the ceiling; on the left-hand side of the room, away from the subdued daylight, colours become richer.

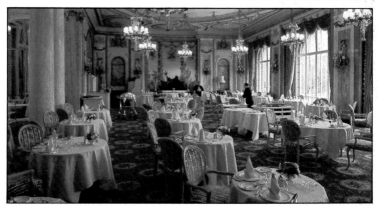

Capture Moving Lights

In fading daylight, and after dark, the camera can record scenes as the eye never sees them – moving lights make swirling trails of colour on the film. Cars and other traffic, especially, leave tell-tale traces: continuous bands of white and red from their head and tail lights, and broken splashes of amber from their directional indicators.

● **Set the camera to 'B',** the bulb setting, for slower shutter speeds. This holds the shutter open while the shutter release is depressed. Exposures lasting minutes, or even hours, are possible.

● **Work at dusk or dawn** if you can. At these times there is still a little light in the sky, so your pictures will come out with a brilliant blue backdrop.

● **Most automatic SLR cameras** have a slowest shutter speed of about 30 seconds, so in many instances all that you need to do is set a small aperture, and the shutter speed will automatically be the one that you require.

● **Use slow film.** Despite the dim conditions, you will find that slow film gives you a wider choice of exposures. Colours will be richer with slow film, too.

● **Use a cable release.** Lock it to keep the shutter open – without holding the release down with your thumb.

● **Either use a tripod** if you want to record static objects without blur, or …

● **… Hand-hold the camera,** as I did for the shot below opposite. This makes the whole scene attractively blurred.

● **Guess the exposure.** Take a meter reading first, but do not assume that this will indicate the perfect setting. The sensitivity of film falls in dim light and you should cover a range of exposures if you want to be sure of success.

▼ Daylight film, exposed for four minutes at *f22*, caught the head, fog and hazard lights of a Range Rover as it crossed a darkened moor.

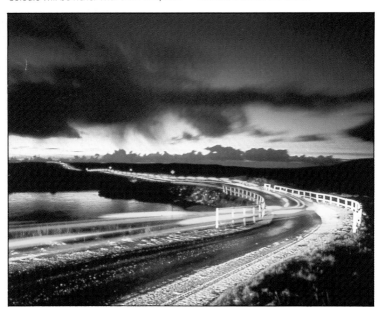

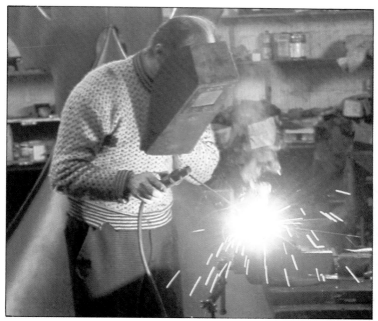

▲ Sparks from a welding torch, shot at 1/30, produce streaks on daylight film, registering yellow as they lose heat.

▼ Neon lights become a pattern of lines by waving the camera about during a two-second exposure at f16.

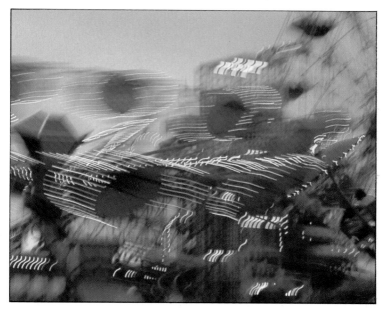

Photograph Flames

Fire has an intrinsic fascination that makes it an excellent subject. Today's film emulsions are so fast that you can use flames as a sole source of illumination at night. By day, fire adds excitement or warmth to both indoor and outdoor scenes.

● **Use any film** if flames appear in the picture. Most film is made to give true colours in daylight, so pictures taken by firelight always look yellow. But our eyes are used to seeing amber flames, so pictures that include fire look quite natural. Tungsten slide film will give slightly weaker yellow and orange tints.

● **Use a filter** if flames light the subject, but do not themselves appear. On daylight film, an 80A filter will retain some of their warmth, but will prevent the colours from looking too heavy.

● **Do not meter the flames,** as they will mislead the exposure meter. Instead, take a reading from the most brightly lit part of the subject.

● **Move the subject nearer** the flames if your meter does not give a high enough shutter-speed reading. Halving the distance between flames and subject quadruples the level of illumination.

● **Use several speeds.** Different speeds can change the appearance of flames dramatically.

▼ A single match provided enough light for the picture below, bringing out warm tones in the girl's face. Candles produce the same effect and are easier to work with. Exposure on ISO 600 tungsten film was 1/15 at *f*4.

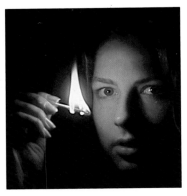

▼ Exposing for a fire-eater's torch has created a silhouette – but increasing exposure, or using flash, would have made the flames hard to see.

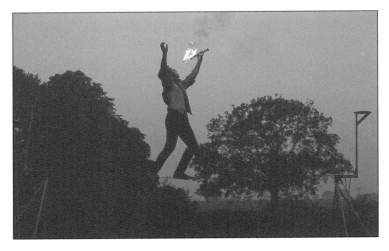

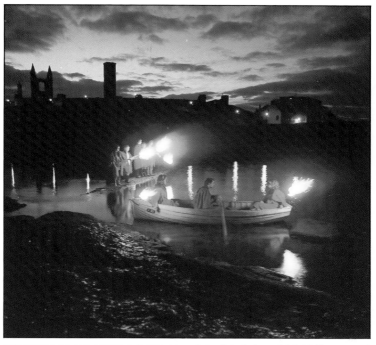

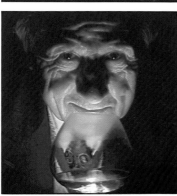

▲ Daylight-balanced ISO 64 film exposed for half a second at *f*4, emphasized the red robes of the Scottish students.

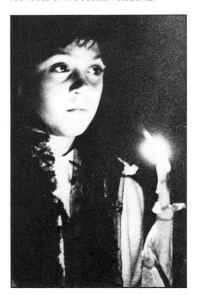

▲ A small torch, shining up through the brandy glass, lit the portrait, with tungsten film giving correct balance to the clothing. Such lighting has to be used carefully to avoid making the subject look sinister.

▶ The girl was lit by a single candle, which created high contrast. The picture was taken on ISO 400 film and its coarse grain can be seen in the result.

Capture Fireworks

Fireworks displays, spectacular when you are a spectator, often prove disappointing on film. The reason is simple. As a spectator you are aware of continuity. In a sense, you retain an after-image of the previous burst of light. But the camera records only what it sees when the shutter is open. To make such displays look as impressive as memory insists they were, you do not need much extra equipment, but you do need to play a few tricks.

● **Estimate exposure** – do not use a meter. As a starting point for a ground-level display set the shutter to 1/30 and divide the film speed by 30 to find the approximate aperture.

● **Use a time exposure** for aerial displays. Keep the shutter open on B by using a cable release and cover the lens with its cap when there is a lull in the proceedings. To select aperture, divide film speed by 10. Be sure to select a good vantage point. You will find that a lens of between 95mm–135mm gives the best results.

● **Use a tripod** and a time exposure if you want silhouettes as a backdrop to the display.

▼ A dozen sparklers were used to create the fiery patterns below.

● **Use flash** in combination with long exposures to catch recognizable views of spectators in front of the display. Try firing several flashes on a single frame.

● **Use sparklers** to trace patterns and outlines during a long exposure. Outlines call for the camera to be mounted on a tripod: dress in dark clothes and follow the edge of an object or a figure with the sparkler. Then fire a flash to fill in detail.

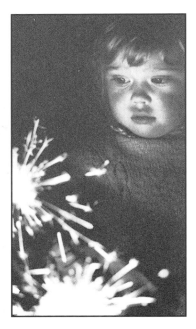

▲ To help with the high contrast in this image, I took a meter reading of the child's face before releasing the shutter.

► The shutter was open for a minute, with the lens covered between explosions, to take the display opposite.

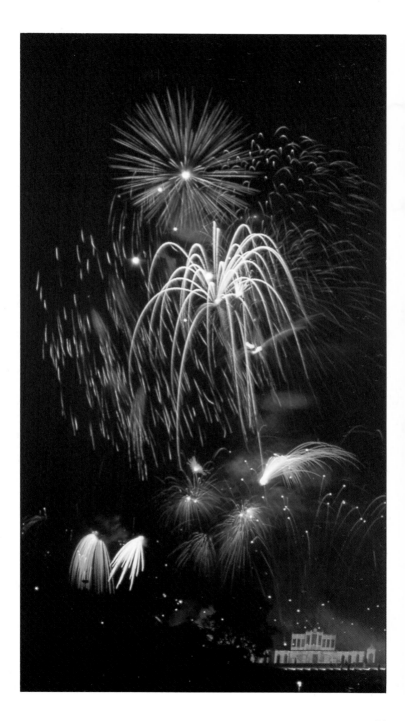

Use stroboscopic Light

Some of photography's most intriguing effects are created by recording a moving subject as a sequence of frozen, overlapping images. You can build such images with a stroboscopic unit, which flashes up to 20 times a second at speeds of up to 1/25,000, or, with an automatic flash-gun.

● **Use** a plain, dark background and make sure that the flash lights only the subject. Black felt is ideal.

● **Keep** the action simple: one subject is enough, at least to start with.

● **Set** the camera on a tripod.

● **Choose** a small aperture to ensure adequate depth of field.

● **Use** the same procedure to calculate the aperture as for using a single flash.

● **Use** a locking cable release to keep the shutter open on the B setting.

● **Fire the flash-gun** at intervals determined by the subject. A slow dance movement may look best with, say, eight flashes over ten seconds.

● **Put coloured filters** on two or more flash-guns to obtain more colourful effects.

● **For really fast action,** you should use a true strobe unit.

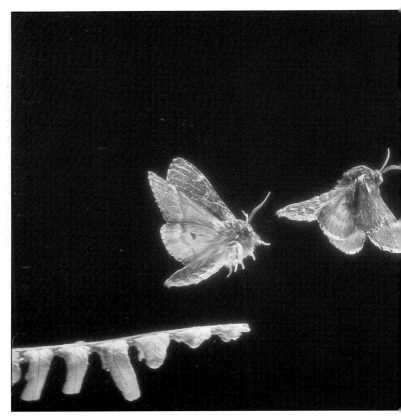

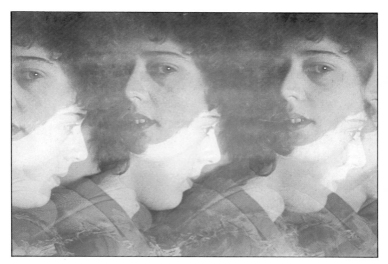

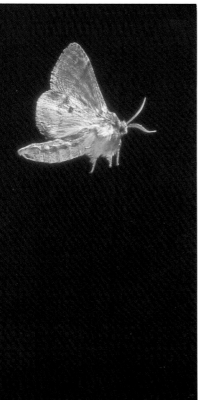

▲ Four flash units synchronized at ten flashes a second were fired during a two-second exposure as the girl walked in front of the camera, turned, and ran back.

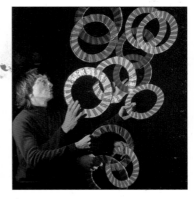

▲ Images like this can be taken with a single automatic flashgun by pressing the flash's 'test' button several times while the camera's shutter is locked open using the 'B' setting.

◀ A strobe lamp was fired every 1/125 of a second for 1/25,000 of a second to capture the movement of the moth flying in a glass corridor.

Take Pictures in Zoos

Nature provides millions of subjects, ranging from domestic pets to underwater plants, and in this section of the book you will find ways of capturing them on film. Zoos are a good place to start. Zoo animals are often cleaner and sleeker than their free-roaming counterparts and with a little ingenuity you can conceal the bars, glass and concrete.

● **Use shadows** and sunlight. Wait until the animal moves into a pool of light, then frame it against an area of shadow. The dark background will disguise the surroundings.

● **Pick your moment.** Many zoo animals alternate between periods of frenetic activity and bored pacing around their pen.

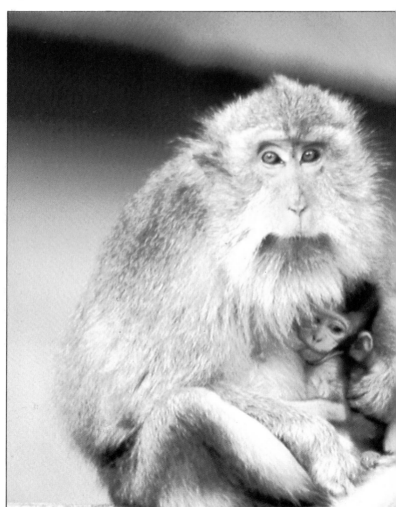

● **Try panning.** Set a slow shutter speed and pan to follow a moving animal (see page 86). This makes the background a series of abstract streaks.

● **Use a wide aperture** and press your lens close to the glass, bars or mesh. The shallow depth of field will disguise the barrier.

● **Close in** with a long telephoto lens or teleconverter. The narrow angle of view means that small patches of foliage will make an adequate background, and the telephoto's shallow depth of field will soften and hide any obtrusive background detail.

▼ A 250mm lens, set at its maximum aperture of *f*4, kept the baby monkey and its mother sharp, but blurred an obtrusive background, softening detail and helping to create an overall harmony of colour.

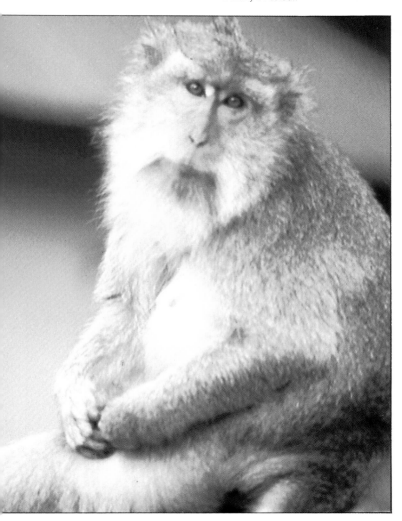

Close in on Plants

Plants are the simplest of natural subjects to photograph in close-up. As they stay rooted in one place, you can take all the time that is necessary to obtain the best possible picture. And since many plants are quite large, you do not always need elaborate close-up equipment in order to fill the frame.

● **Use close-up lenses** for larger plants. These lenses are cheap and attach to the front of your regular lens.

● **For tiny objects** use a macro lens or extension tubes. Although quite costly, these produce high-quality results.

● **Protect plants** from wind by using a wind break or your body.

● **Use a reflector** to fill in the shadows and reduce contrast.

● **Greater exposure** than usual is needed for extreme close-ups, because of the increased distance between the lens-front and the film. On most cameras, this happens automatically with bellows units and extension tubes, but for older cameras check exposure compensation tables. No compensation is needed for close-up lenses.

● **Use a tripod** and cable release to minimize camera shake.

● **Stop the lens down** to maximize depth of field.

● **Use fast film** for flash to help overcome the problems of depth of field or movement.

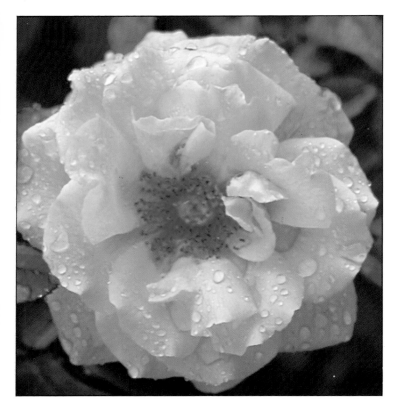

► Subjects as large as this lily do not usually present too much of a problem. A shutter speed of 1/125 and an aperture of f16 with a 70–200mm zoom lens were sufficient to freeze the subject and fill the frame.

▼ An early start was necessary to capture the frost gleaming from these autumnal leaves, which a 50mm macro lens has isolated.

◄ For this rose I used a close-up lens: but that depth of field was not enough to render the whole bloom in focus.

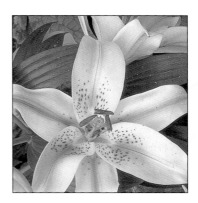

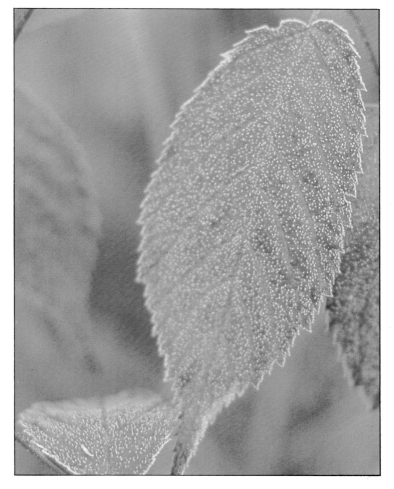

Photograph Wildlife

Wild animals present special photographic problems: the biggest difficulty is getting close enough to the beasts to fill the frame of the viewfinder.

A hide like the one pictured below makes this very much easier, but there are a number of techniques that you need to master if you are to avoid photographing only the vanishing tail of your quarry.

● **Use a long lens setting:** you may be able to get away with 200mm, but a 400mm lens setting is better. Buy the lens with the widest maximum aperture that you can afford, so that you can throw distracting backgrounds out of focus if necessary.

● **Fast film** allows faster shutter speeds with limited apertures to retain depth of field. Slow film can be used in bright sunlight, or if your subject is fairly approachable.

● **Know your subject.** The more you know about the animal's habitat and behaviour, the simpler it is to approach and photograph it without disturbing it.

● **You should stay downwind** of your quarry. Animals have a highly developed sense of smell.

● **Use a hide.** This can be as simple as a blanket over your head, with a hole cut for the lens.

● **Lay bait.** You will be surprised at the range of wildlife that appears if you put out bait regularly. The fox, below, was wary and difficult to photograph, so I let out some chickens (rescued in time), the fox became intent on the chase.

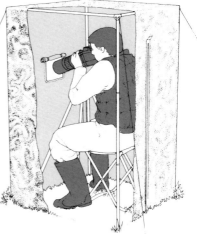

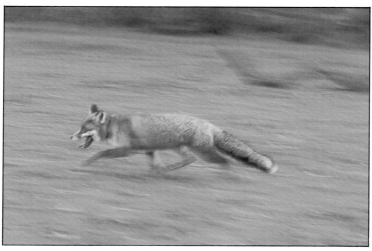

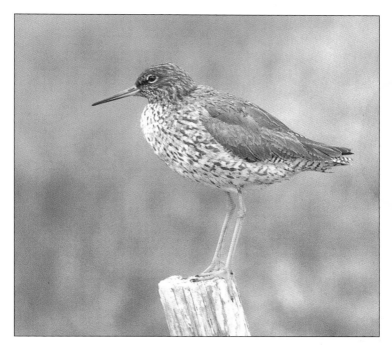

▲ Even using a hide and a 400mm lens, it was essential to use the maximum available aperture of f5.6 to make sure that this redshank stood out clearly against the background.

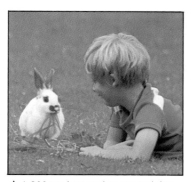

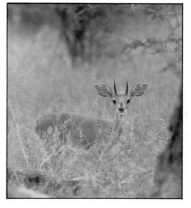

▲ A 200mm lens setting ensured that the camera did not disturb boy or rabbit. Be patient with animals: it may take several hours before your subject appears and is at ease in your presence. Make yourself comfortable and keep low so that you are below the horizon.

▲ The best wildlife pictures always show the animal in its natural habitat. Selective focusing helps to pick out animals from a background that provides them with natural camouflage, as in this shot of an impala, taken with a 400mm lens. Always put animals before photographs – remember that if you come too close to an animal's lair you could force it to abandon its young.

Close in on Nature

Insects and small animals can be especially difficult to photograph. Close-up work offers problems of focus, depth of field and lighting. These are greater when the subject might dive into a pond or dart into the undergrowth. You may need to use bait to tempt an animal to sit still for a minute or two, or move away and use a motor drive operated by remote control.

● **Use a long focus lens** – either a telephoto with extension tubes or a 100mm or 200mm macro lens. This will enable you to fill the frame from a greater distance, and thus avoid disturbing your subject.

● **Wait** until the animal settles down before taking the photograph. Animals feed only when they are relaxed: you can be fairly sure that an animal that is eating will ignore the sound of the camera shutter.

● **Move** the camera for accurate focus rather than turning the focusing ring or using autofocus. By moving back and forth you can focus more quickly with equal accuracy.

● **Confine your subject** in an aquarium or in a box. By limiting the animal's movement in this way you have more control over it, and over other factors such as the lighting and the background.

● **Cold-blooded animals** move more quickly when they are warm, so early in the day – before they become warm – may prove the easiest time to find and photograph them.

▶ Underexposing by half a stop helps to increase colour saturation in close-up photographs. It pays to load with fast film to ensure a sufficient depth of field.

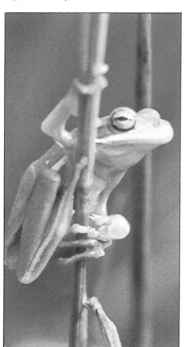

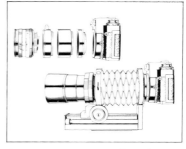

▲ When the camera-to-subject distance is too short, focusing with a standard lens is impossible. An extension tube or a set of bellows between the camera and the lens, allows you to focus closely enough to get an image on film that is as large as the subject itself. Special macro lenses tend to give maximum image magnifications of half life-size.

◀ The characteristic problem of close-up photography is the very limited depth of field, even with small apertures, which becomes more restricted the closer you focus.

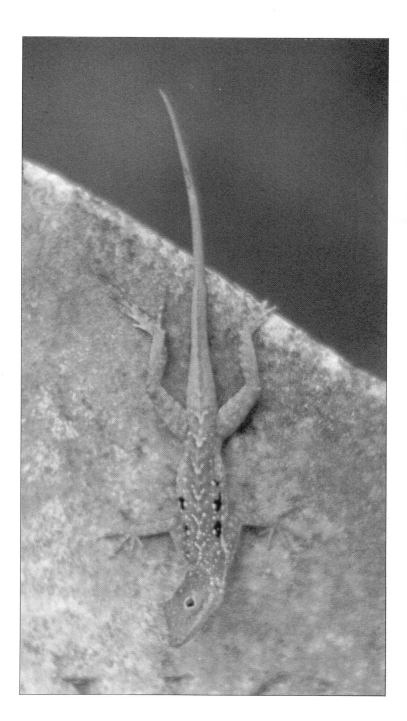

Stop Birds on the Wing

Birds in flight are difficult to photograph, calling for impeccable camera craft and fast reactions. However, if you know enough about the habits of one bird and use the technique below, you can overcome the problems.

● **Set up the camera** near the bird's flight path. This is easiest when the bird is nesting, because most birds returning to a nest will perch on a particular branch some distance from it and look around, before finally approaching it.

● **Focus on one point** through which you know, from watching, that the bird will fly (see pages 84–85).

● **Set up a flash unit** to light the bird in flight. Use it on its manual setting and find the correct exposure by testing. Two units will make the light look more natural.

● **Automate camera firing** – so that the bird takes a self-portrait – by using a special infrared trigger. When the bird flies through the beam of infrared light, the flash and the camera are fired.

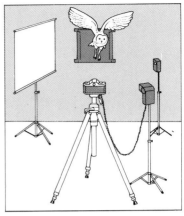

▲ Weak daylight, fill-in flash, and 1/25 enabled me to blur the wings of the owl. Always put the bird first – never threaten its health or interrupt its breeding cycle.

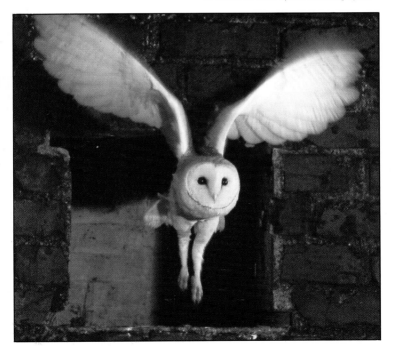

Record Aquarium Life

Underwater photography does not necessarily mean using diving gear and an underwater camera. With access to an aquarium, you can photograph fish with your regular camera in conditions over which you have control.

● **Divide the tank** with sheets of glass (right). The glass is invisible, but will keep the fish close to the camera.

● **Move the camera as close** to the tank as possible to eliminate reflections of the room behind.

● **Position a flash-gun** above the tank or to one side. Flash stops movement and lets you use a small aperture, so focusing is not as critical.

● **Improve the setting.** Card or plastic behind the tank will change the background colour.

● **Use backlighting** to show the translucent bodies of some small fish.

● **Turn out the room lights** but use a table lamp above the tank to aid focusing. A darkened room helps to prevent reflections.

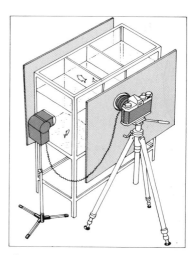

▲ Make sure the glass of the tank is clean and the water clear. Fit a polarizing filter to minimize reflections and do not use photofloods – they heat the water.

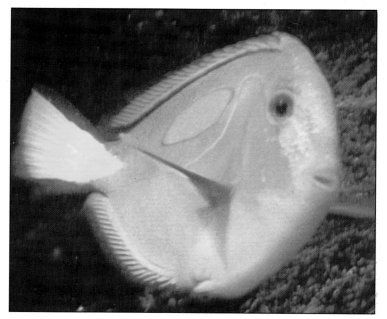

Pre-focus on Action

Action photography may seem fraught with difficulties: stop the action with a a fast shutter speed and you lose the impression of movement; fail to do so and blur may make the subject unrecognizable. How, if you want to photograph a spectator sport, do you get close enough for impact? How do you cope with fast movement in low light? How do you focus on a moving subject? If the action is dangerous, or too far away for you to get close to it, or confined behind barriers, what do you do? The next 10 pages deal with these problems, beginning with that of focusing. One answer is to set the focus in advance and to wait until the subject is sharp before releasing the shutter.

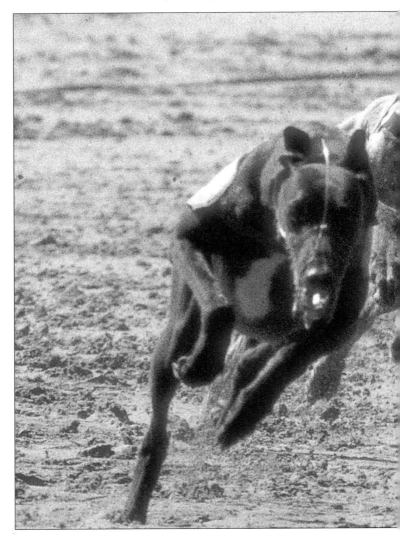

● **Select your viewpoint** with care. Many subjects almost stop at some point and by pre-focusing on this particular spot you can choose your moment more easily. For example, someone jumping up is practically stationary at the top of the leap.

● **Press the shutter release** an instant before the subject reaches the point of sharpest focus. There is always a short delay between pressing the release and the opening of the shutter.

● **Practise** with unimportant subjects on black-and-white film. Do not bother with prints – check focusing accuracy on the negatives with a magnifier.

▼ Pre-focusing on the corner and a speed of 1/2000 has stopped these greyhounds in their tracks.

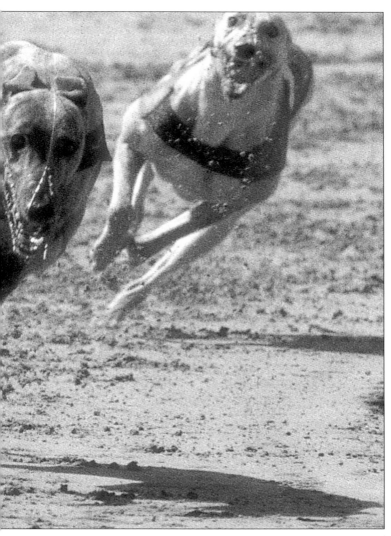

Pan with the Action

Panning – swinging it to follow a moving object – gives the photographer a unique way to represent movement. Using this technique, a single photograph can incorporate both a crisp image of the speeding subject and a background of impressionistic streaks that sweep the viewer's eye across the frame. Because panning simply involves smooth, controlled movement of the camera, special equipment is unnecessary – the technique is equally suitable whether you own a cheap snapshot camera or a sophisticated SLR.

● **Stand where the subject** will pass directly across the camera's field of view. Do not stand too close, for safety reasons and because, if the action fills the frame, you will find it hard to avoid cropping off bits of the subject. At its closest, the subject should cover no more than half the width of the frame.

● **Stand comfortably** with your legs apart. Make sure that you can move freely to both left and right.

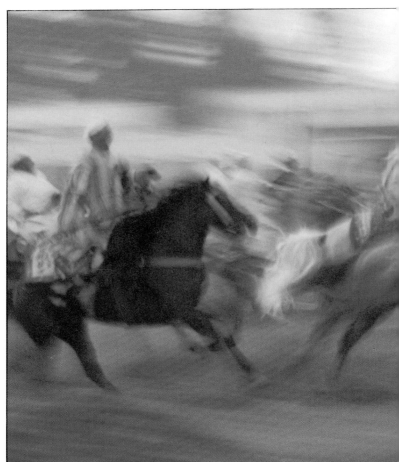

● **Pre-focus the camera** where you expect the subject to be when you press the shutter. You'll have one less thing to worry about at the moment of exposure.

● **Frame the subject** as soon as it appears in the distance, but resist the temptation to refocus.

● **Choose a slow shutter** speed – 1/16 to 1/15 – and release the shutter smoothly just before the subject is ideally positioned.

● **Turn your whole body** from the waist – do not just turn the camera – and follow through by tracking the receding subject. Do not just stop as soon as you hear the shutter fire, or the panning action will be less smooth.

● **Practise panning** by standing at the edge of a busy road and following the cars. Start without film, then load the camera as soon as you are more confident of your panning skills.

● **Watch the background.** Plain backgrounds tend to reduce the impression of movement. Avoid light backgrounds, as these may cause a kind of ghost image on the picture.

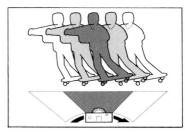

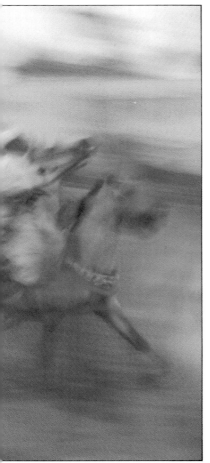

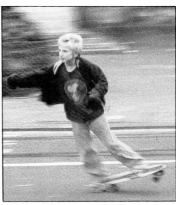

▲ As shown in the diagram, a pan should begin some distance before the button is pressed and continue after exposure is completed.

◄ I used a slow shutter speed (1/15) to intensify the action of these galloping Berbers. Faster moving subjects, such as racing cars, will need a faster shutter speed (up to 1/250) as well as a more rapid panning action.

Close in on Action

Telephoto lenses get you close enough to fill the frame in difficult or dangerous situations. They also dramatically compress the middle and far distances, which adds impact to distant subjects.

● **Use a 200mm or longer lens setting** to create pictures that feature compressed space.

● **Use fast film** with long zoom lenses because the maximum aperture on most is *f*4 or *f*5.6.

● **Stop down** if possible. Depth of field can be very limited.

● **Support the camera** with a monopod to avoid camera shake.

● **Use fast shutter speeds,** particularly if you are hand-holding the camera.

▼ The dramatic picture of a firejump was taken with a 400mm lens. Without using it, I could not have got close enough to the subject.

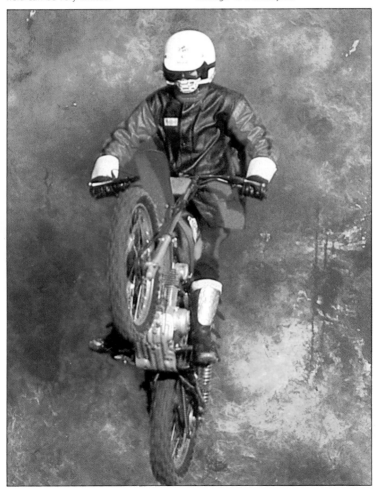

Zoom in on Action

Changing the focal length of a zoom lens during the exposure creates a tunnel of lines converging on the centre of the frame. Used with discretion, this technique can add pep to a mundane subject and excitement and action to an otherwise static scene.

● **Set a slow shutter speed,** ie 1/8 or 1/4, so that you have time to operate the zoom while the shutter is open.

● **Use a small aperture** with automatic or program exposure models. The camera will select a slow shutter speed.

● **Add grey filters** (neutral density) if bright sun and fast film will not let you set a slow enough shutter speed.

● **Frame the picture** with an obvious part of the subject at the centre of the viewfinder– the rest will be streaked.

● **Use colour film.** Zoom effects can look drab in black and white.

● **Start to zoom** before you press the shutter, keeping the movement smooth to mimimize camera shake. Do not stop zooming as soon as the shutter is fired.

● **Crop the print** so to avoid the converging lines meeting at the centre. Precise symmetry can be disconcerting.

▼ The best 'speed lines' result from a .picture with a background in which highlights and shadows mix.

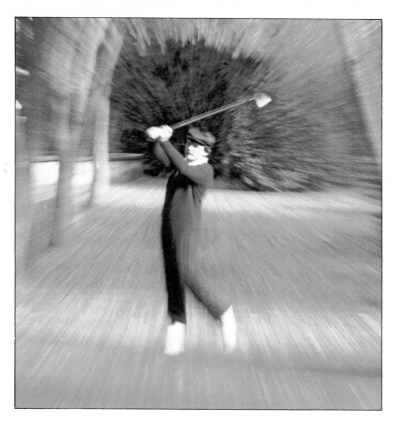

Freeze Fast Action

Some of today's cameras have shutter speeds as fast as 1/8000 of a second – and if you are prepared to pay a high price for a high speed, you will get a camera that will freeze most action. But even with more modest equipment you can still get sharp pictures of rapidly moving subjects by taking the steps suggested here.

● **Roll with the action.** When moving at the same speed as the subject – as I was for the shot of the water skier below – the negligible relative movement lets you use 1/1000, a speed all SLRs have.

● **Use fast film** in dull conditions, which will let you select a fast speed.

● **Use electronic flash** if the subject is near you. Doing this will arrest all movement (see page 58).

● **Choose camera angles carefully.** An advancing or retreating subject is can be frozen with a much slower shutter speed than one crossing the field of view.

● **Keep your distance.** Objects can appear almost static a long way off.

▼ A shutter speed of 1/500 froze the boy and ball below. This shot called for skilful timing.

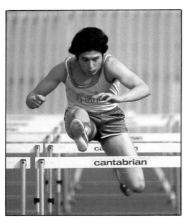

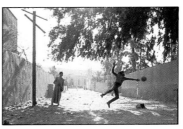

◄ Choose the right moment to take the picture. I used a zoom with a 400mm lens setting to catch the hurdler in flight.

▼ The water skier was taken from the towing boat with a 135mm lens setting

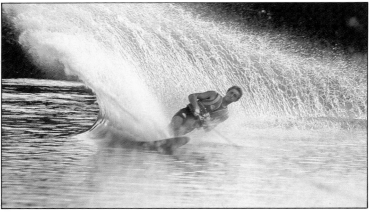

Use Remote Control

Motor drives are now built into the majority of modern SLRs – advancing the film and cocking the shutter automatically after each shot. If linked to a remote control system, a motor drive gives you a better chance of taking the perfect action picture and lets you take as many as you like without going near the camera.

● **Use remote control** to get two views of the same event. Set a motor-driven camera on a tripod in one position and trigger it from where you stand with a second camera.

● **Use a cable** with a simple push-to-close switch for the most reliable remote-control connection.

● **Set focus manually.** Even if your camera has autofocus, focus manually onto the area that you are training the camera on. An autofocus is likely to focus on the background if you are not there to point the focus window at the subject when it comes into view.

● **Avoid radio control** because stray radio transmissions can fire your shutter prematurely. Use an electric cable or an infrared release system.

▼ A remote control unit allows you to get your camera close to the action without risking your own safety.

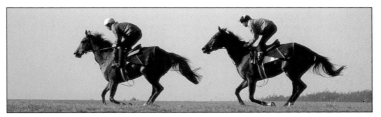

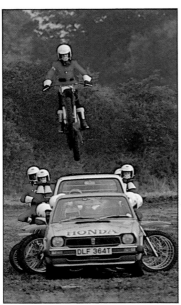

▼ Pre-planning is essential in taking several pictures of the same piece of action. In this case I chose my viewpoints well in advance and used remote control to trigger two of the three cameras that I was using.

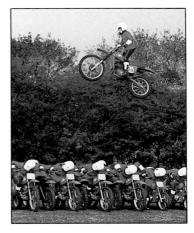

Light Indoor Sport

Unless you are at a large sports arena, it is likely that any indoor sport that you shoot is going to involve working at very low light levels. The question that you should ask yourself is whether to make the best of the ambient illumination or to supplement the lighting with a flash-gun.

● **Flash-guns are banned** at many indoor arenas as the light can put off the competitors and may irritate the other spectators, so check before shooting.

● **Using the fastest film** that you can find will mean that you can still take pictures in the dingiest conditions. ISO 3200 colour print and black-and-white films can be bought.

● **If you need faster shutter speeds** than are suggested by your camera's meter you can 'push' your film. Pushing means deliberately underexposing the film by choosing an ISO setting that is one or two stops greater than that recommended by the maker. This underexposure can then be corrected by overdeveloping the film at the processing stage.

● **Flash can be used** when you want to increase the contrast in the picture by livening up the drab, even illumination in the sports hall. However, you must make sure that you are close enough to your subject for it to have an effect. Flash can also eliminate distracting backgrounds by throwing them into relative darkness in the picture.

● **A long shutter speed**, such as 1/8, combined with flash, will record both a sharp image and a gentle blurring that suggests the excitement of the activity.

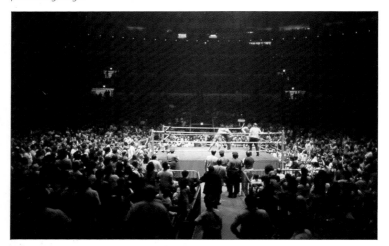

▲ Sometimes a general shot of the auditorium tells you more about the event than a close-up of the action. Also, the wide maximum aperture available on a standard lens, coupled with fast film, allows you the freedom of taking advantage of available light for your shots.

▶ The picture of the gymnast was lit from the rear right by a strong spotlight that established a suitable atmosphere. I added an electronic flash from the same direction and another unit at front left. An exposure of 1/30 picked out background flare and using flash froze the movement.

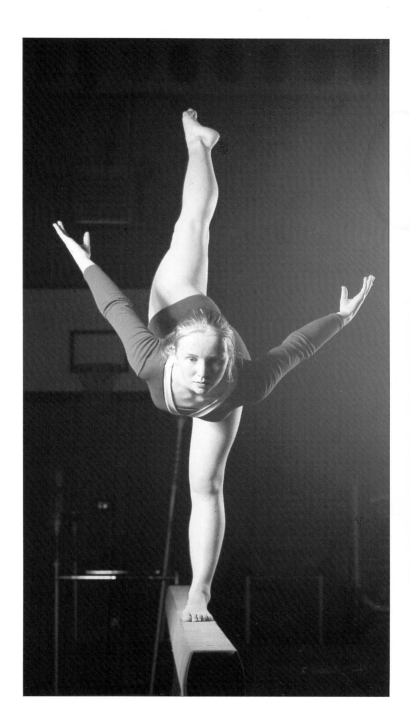

Show a Sweeping Vista

Landscapes, seemingly among the easiest of subjects, have their own special difficulties, dealt with in the pages that follow. The fundamental difficulty is of capturing on film the majesty that delights the eye. Because the eye views a scene by constantly sweeping it (and changing focus), reason suggests that a wide-angle lens might be the answer. But, in fact, to get a similar field of view, you would have to use several lenses. The right answer is to see landscapes with a painterly eye and be selective.

● **Evaluate the scene** before even getting out your camera. Decide exactly what it is that gives the landscape its charm and then consider how you can best bring out those particular qualities. Don't just take a snapshot.

● **Close in on a part** of the scene that sums up the whole image. A telephoto lens (as I used in the shot below) is often more useful than a wide-angle lens.

● **Blow up the negative** or slide to a scale that does justice to the grandeur of the original scene. Part of the awe-inspiring nature of landscape lies in turning your head to scan the view. A large print allows its viewer to experience the scene just as you did when photographing it.

● **Use the panoramic mode** that is available on many of today's cameras. These crop pictures top and bottom for you as you take them, providing a format that ideally suits the long, stretched-out proportions of many vistas. If you do not have this facility, your prints can be trimmed top and bottom after processing.

Capture Dawn and Dusk

Dawn and dusk make irresistible subjects for the camera: shades of russet, azure, pink and gold demand your attention. And although the huge contrasts between dark and light are often too great for any film to copy accurately, there is much you can do to make your pictures more colourful and dramatic.

● **Meter from the sky,** not from the ground or from the sun.

● **Bracket your pictures** (three stops should be enough). It is hard to know which setting will give the best results.

● **Work quickly** if you want to catch the sun actually touching the horizon. The closer you are to the equator, the more quickly the sun rises and sets.

● **Use fill-in flash** to retain detail in the immediate foreground. Strong backlighting will otherwise create silhouettes (see page 60).

● **Slide film** records the intensity and vibrancy of colours more accurately than print film.

● **Check in the papers** to find the times of sunrise and sunset – then you can make sure that you have a few minutes to prepare.

● **Use a compass** to note the direction of the sun at dawn or dusk the day before. The following day you will be able to set up in the best position.

Contrary to popular opinion, the sun only rises due east or set due west twice a year – the direction of sunrise and sunset varies in an arc of up to 90°, depending on the time of year.

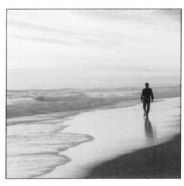

▲ Water was used to reflect and intensify the delicate colours of the sky just before dawn.

▼ Failing light at dusk reduces the enclosing hills to silhouettes, while detail in the town is maintained by the green glow of fluorescent street lighting stretched along the waterfront.

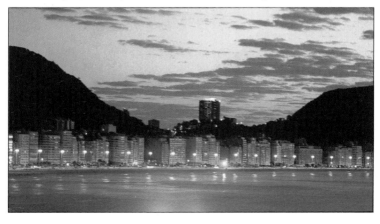

► Take a reading from a weak or setting sun about 25° off centre and vary exposure a stop either side.

▼ Shots that include the setting sun can have dramatic impact if taken with a long-focus lens. This type of lens tends to squash perspective, making any object in the background loom larger than it would normally appear. With shots like this, bracket your exposures.

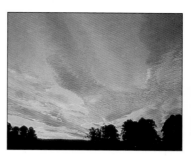

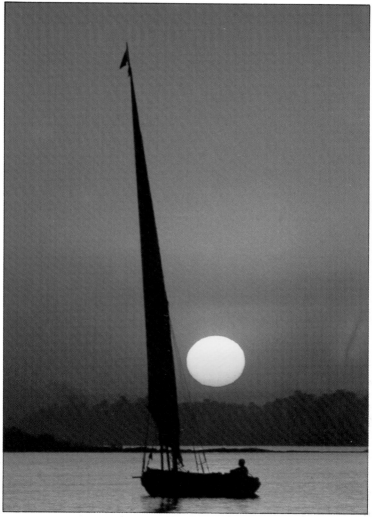

Freeze and Blur Water

Like a flickering flame, a body of moving water has the capacity to hypnotize the viewer. On film, water is just as fascinating – altering the shutter speed enables you to record running water as being silky smooth and floating or as hard and sharp as crystal.

● **Use fast shutter speeds** – the fastest ones your camera offers – to record water as clearly defined, glassy splashes. In sunlight the water will sparkle, and you should still be able to set a reasonably small aperture for extended depth of field.

● **Use slow shutter speeds** – five seconds or more – to make running water seem to float like a soft mist. Even with slow film and the smallest aperture you still may not get a slow enough shutter speed. If this is the case, use a neutral density filter. These are essentially grey glass or plastic filters that cut down the amount of light entering the lens. An 8 x ND filter will require three stops more exposure than usual at a given light level, and is ideal for this type of photography.

● **More lifelike results** are obtained using speeds of 1/60 or 1/125. At these speeds the water is recorded almost as it appears as you see the scene.

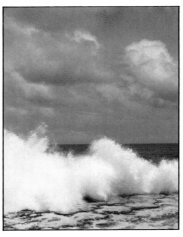

▲ Quick reflexes and an observant eye are necessary to capture waves crashing onto the shore.

▼ A shutter speed of 1/250 has been sufficient to freeze the swimmer, but not the splashes of water.

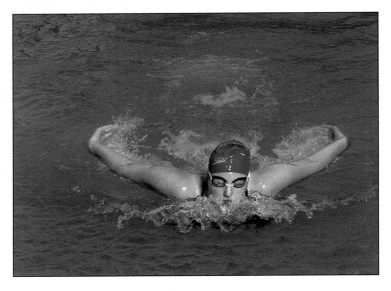

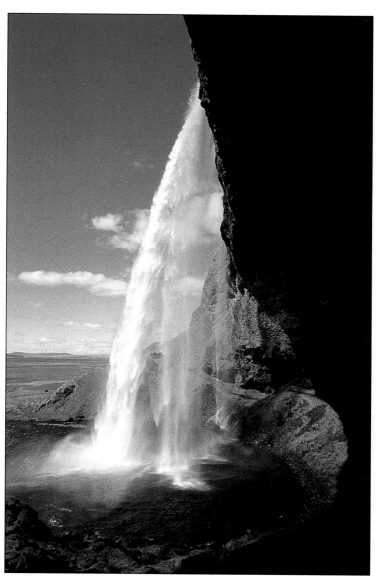

▲ By walking round this giant waterfall I was able to select the best camera position to capture it on film. Setting up my SLR on a tripod to the side of the cascading water, I could use sidelighting to accentuate the highlights on the spray.

Intensify Colours

Colourful landscapes do not always make brilliantly coloured photographs as haze or sun flare can bleach the brightest scene. a few simple precautions will allow you to record colours as rich and pure as they appeared to the eye.

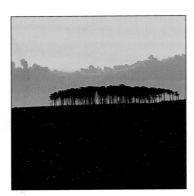

▲ By underexposing this shot by one full stop, I have accentuated the purple hue of the sky.

● **Use a lens hood** to remove non-image-forming light.

● **Colours are richest** in the early morning or late afternoon with the sun behind the camera. Top-lighting weakens colour.

● **Underexpose** by about half a stop when using slide film in order to brighten the colours.

● **A polarizing filter** cuts out glare from the surface of water or foliage, making hues look cleaner and purer. Rotate the filter and note the strongest result as you look through the lens.

▼ A polarizing filter was used to cut out reflections and intensify the colour in this aerial shot of a coral reef.

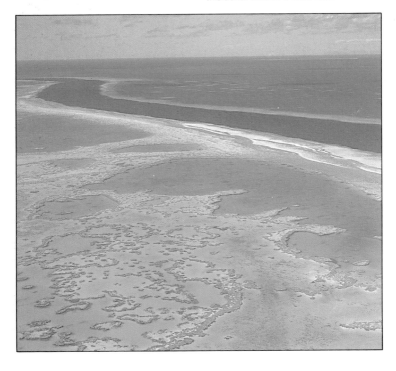

Photograph Skies

Every photographer knows that dramatic skies make for dramatic landscapes, yet very few seem to point their cameras upwards and make the sky the subject of the picture. If the weather is windy, the sky will be constantly in motion, so even if you just stay in the same place you will be presented with an infinite variety of changing patterns and lighting effects.

● **Use filters** to add drama to the scene and to increase colour saturation. A polarizing filter will make a blue sky look bluer and darker without affecting the colour of the clouds, so strengthening contrast.

● **Bracket your pictures** by making a series of exposures using different apertures or shutter speeds. Often you will find that over- or underexposed pictures have more impact than ones taken at the 'correct' exposure.

● **Watch the weather** and do not be discouraged by rain and storms. The air is much clearer just after rain, and colours more intense.

● **Get up early** or go out late. The sky is generally more spectacular during the first and last three hours of the day.

● **Try black-and-white film** with a red filter. A blue sky will turn black, accentuating clouds and bringing the sense of an impending summer storm.

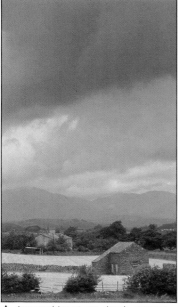

▲ Approaching storm clouds contrast vividly with the sparkling hues of green and gold in the landscape below.

► The glowing colours and extra-ordinary definition of this rainbow contrast well with the plain greys of the rain clouds.

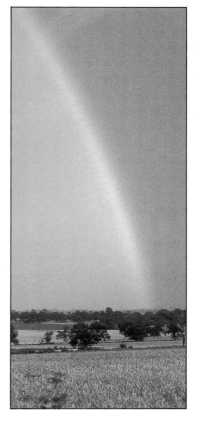

Make Snow look White

Snow transforms the landscape, but the brilliant white mantle can present special problems to the photographer. Careful control of exposure and colour rendition is essential if the snow is not to reflect colour from its surroundings.

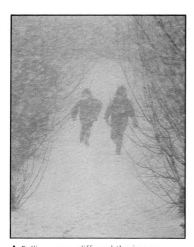

● **Meter carefully.** The brightness of the reflected light can mislead your camera's built-in meter. There are three ways to avoid this:

● **Close in** on the main subject so that snow does not fill the frame. Meter, set the exposure manually, and then move back to recompose the picture.

● **With a hand-held meter,** measure the light that falls on the scene, rather than that reflected. This is an incident light reading – point the meter's diffusing dome at the camera from the subject position. Keep footprints out of the image area.

● **Overexpose** – set the film speed on the camera to half that of your film, and bracket shots.

▲ Falling snow diffused the image of the two boys. I took the picture through a closed window with a 400mm lens. Exposure was 1/250 at f8 on Ektachrome 200.

▼ In contrast, I used a 100mm macro lens for the picture of frost-rimed trees against a misty sky. The exposure, just sufficient to reveal detail, was 1/250 at f5.6 on Ektachrome 64.

● **Filter carefully.** Snow picks up colour casts more easily than other scenes. In overcast weather use an 81C filter, and when the sky is blue and the scene totally in shadow, use an 81EF filter. In bright sunlight no filter should be necessary. A polarizing filter will cut out any glare.

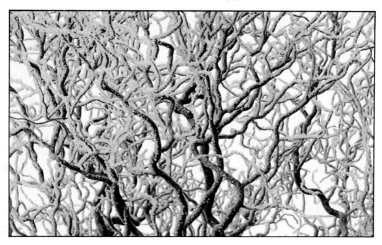

Take Aerial Landscapes

From the air the countryside takes on a new perspective. Hedges and trees shrink to small lines and dots, and the whole panorama becomes a tapestry of colour and abstract pattern, spreading out beneath you in all directions.

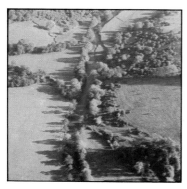

▲ Shadows and form, created by oblique light, make this aerial shot realistic, not abstract.

▼ Seen from above, terraced rice fields reveal strong patterns through the interplay between light and colour.

● **Commercial aircraft** have a perspex inner layer inside the window glass. Any dirt on the windows may appear on the picture. Press the lens against the window and use a large aperture.

● **Avoid long telephoto lenses,** as they are impossible to hold steady enough to avoid image blur caused by the aircraft's engines. Focal lengths from 35mm–105mm are ideal.

● **Use a fast shutter speed** – this will help to keep camera shake at bay.

● **Shoot just after take-off** and before landing – at lower altitudes there are fewer problems with haze.

● **Ask about helicopter rides** and plane trips when you are visiting a new city or attraction.

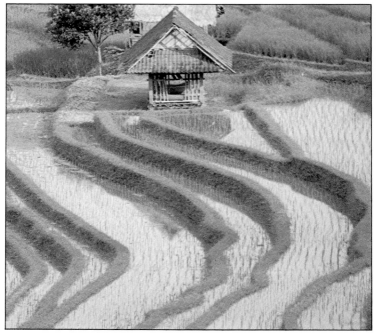

Exploit Haze and Mist

Even on clear days, the atmosphere contains particles of dust and water vapour that make the horizon appear bluer and paler than the foreground. On film, this produces an effect of depth which you can manipulate and exaggerate to add to the sense of three dimensions in your pictures.

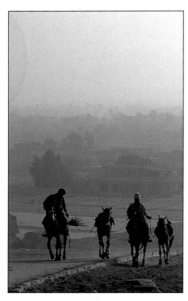

● **Use a telephoto lens** or a teleconverter. This will magnify the misty portion of a scene.

● **Shoot late in the day** when a low sun exaggerates mist. Early in the morning you may catch mist where it gathers in hollows.

● **Use a pale blue filter** to emphasize the natural blueness of haze and mist. With black-and-white film a deep blue filter can be equally effective.

● **Find foreground detail** and position it prominently in the frame. This will contrast the pale blue distance with the harder lines of the nearby object.

● **Avoid** side lighting as it tends to reduce haze and mist to a minimum.

● **Remove** the UV filter if you keep one on your lens as it reduces the blueness of the haze.

▲ Haze can help to accentuate the depth in a landscape – as objects farther from the camera become gradually less and less distinct. This effect is known as aerial perspective.

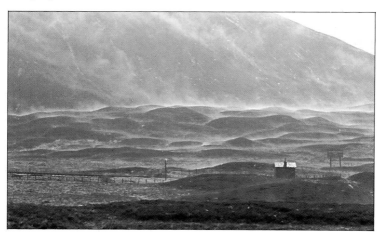

Control Scale and Size

The photographer's golden rule that 'telephotos compress space and wide-angle lenses expand it' is really only partially true. The factor that affects perspective is your distance from the subject; it is simply that wide-angle lenses tend to be used closer to their main subject than telephotos.

● **Pick a close viewpoint** to exaggerate size relationships. From close up, even small objects loom larger than more distant objects – however big the latter may be. If it is important to take in the whole of the nearby object, you may have to use a wide-angle lens: this explains the common misconception that wide-angle lenses expand perspective.

● **Pick a distant viewpoint** to portray size relationships as they really are. In the picture on the right, for example, the trees are dominated by the mountain behind. From a close camera position, the mountains would have looked smaller in relation to the trees. To fill the frame with a distant subject, a telephoto lens may be necessary – so it is easy to make the assumption that it is the lens, not the viewpoint, that is the sole influence on scale.

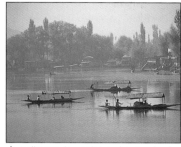

▲ A distant viewpoint and a standard lens have rendered a very natural sense of scale and size in this shot.

▼ I used a close viewpoint and a wide-angle lens (below left) to exaggerate the apparent convergence of the ploughed furrows. By angling the camera down (below), the nearer subjects appear larger than they otherwise would.

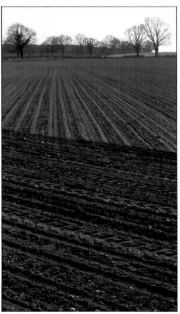

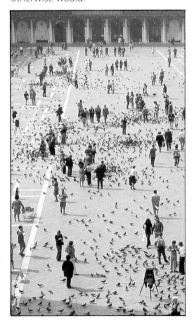

Cope with the Elements

Weather not only affects the subjects you are photographing, it also affects your equipment and film. Humidity and extremes of temperature will produce mould on camera bodies, run down batteries, cloud lenses and alter the colour balance of film.

In rain ...
● **Put your camera** in a plastic bag, with a hole cut for the lens. Protect the lens with a UV filter.

● **Dry the camera** as soon as possible and do not touch film with wet hands.

In the cold ...
● **Keep batteries warm.** Put a spare set in an inside pocket and keep the camera warm under a coat.

● **Use zoom lenses** to minimize the number of changes of lens.

In the heat ...
● **Do not leave your camera** in the open, behind a window or on a car dashboard. Extreme heat may damage cameras and lenses.

● **Refrigerate film** and carry only as much as you need for a day.

● **Process film promptly.**
In the tropics ...

● **Pack all your equipment** in plastic bags with silica gel.

● **When moving** between cool, air-conditioned buildings and outdoors, allow the temperature of the camera to adjust, and condensation to evaporate.

▼ To get good lighting for this rain shot, I used a garden hose in the summer sun.

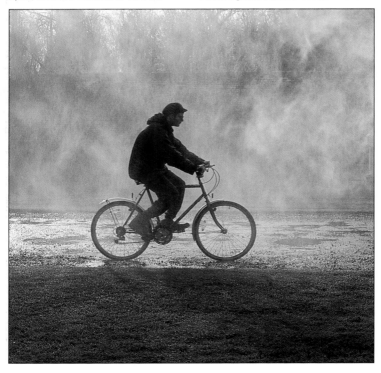

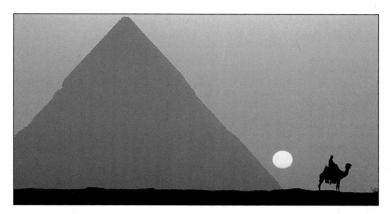

▲ Sand is one of a camera's greatest enemies in the desert or on a beach. Fit a UV filter and carry the camera in a plastic bag. Clean the camera nightly.

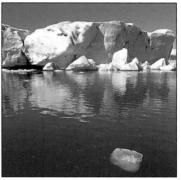

► If possible, take pictures quickly in the cold. Keep the camera covered between shots. Hold your breath in case condensation clouds the lens.

▼ In high humidity, take your camera out of any air-conditioned building half an hour before you want to use it or condensation will form on the lens.

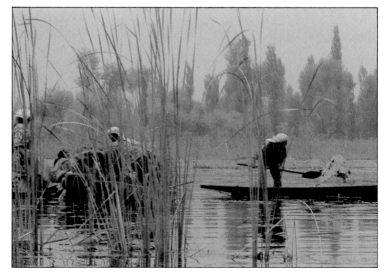

Capture Nightlights

Straightforward photographs of night scenes can be a disappointment – all that appears are dots of light on a black background. To achieve some of the glitter that you see through the viewfinder, use some of the tips below.

● **Shoot at dusk** rather than at night. This will enable you to capture outline details and the colours of the sky rather than just blackness.

● **Move close** to some of the lights, so that they are recorded larger than those farther away. This variation in image size will prevent the lights appearing as a pattern of equal-sized dots.

● **Wait for a wet night.** In wet weather reflections will double the sparkle in the scene.

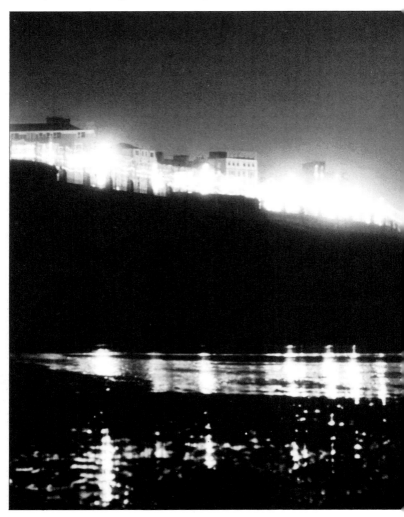

● **Use a long exposure** (15 seconds or more) so that speeding cars leave curving trails of light (see page 66).

● **Try a range of apertures.** You may find that your lens turns the lights into stars at small lens openings.

● **Zoom during exposure,** so that the lights form converging streaks.

● **Gradually defocus** the lens during the course of a time exposure: this will make each light source turn into a soft pool of colour.

● **Fit a starburst** or a diffraction filter. This will form multi-spiked stars from each source of light (see page 129).

▼ An exposure of about one minute at ƒ16 captured Blackpool Tower at night. The most common fault in such pictures is underexposure: deliberate overexposure adds brilliance.

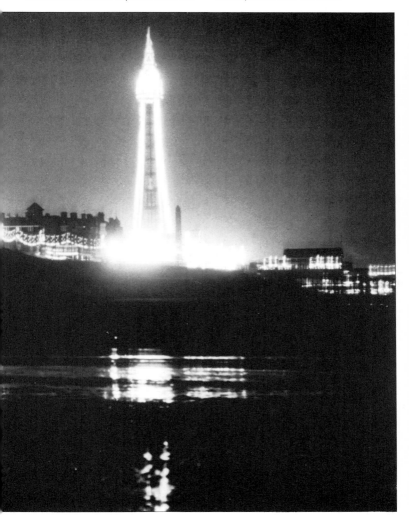

Choose a Viewpoint

Seen from different viewpoints, a building may appear to have several quite varied faces. From close to a single structure will dominate your picture; yet from afar it will have a different relationship with its surroundings.

● **Change scale.** Your subject does not have to fill the frame precisely. In windy weather, for example, clouds speed across the sky, sweeping shafts of light over an otherwise bleak cityscape. Caught in such a fleeting pool of brilliance, a single structure might be spotlighted and drawn out of its surroundings.

● **Use available frames** to draw attention to one particular building. A suitable frame may be another building, a doorway, an arch or a window used to enclose the main subject.

● **Do not stay rooted** in one spot. Changing lenses has no effect on perspective if you stand still. Different focal lengths simply alter how much of the subject your picture takes in.

● **Look up – look down.** The vast majority of photographs are taken from eye level. That is why the other photographs look so unusual. From a worm's-eye view even your garden shed will appear to be a massive, dominating structure.

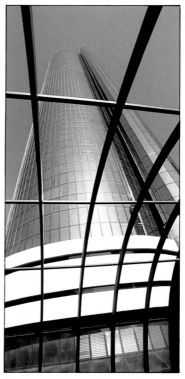

▼ Careful selection of the viewpoint in this shot shows the powerful yet graceful bulk of the windmills in a straightforward way, creating also a strong sense of perspective.

▲ The hard, linear roof struts of a swimming pool make the perfect frame for this shot. A 15mm wide-angle lens ensured adequate depth of field.

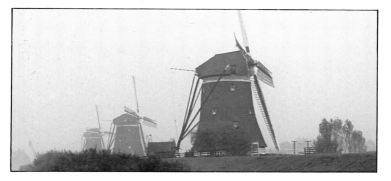

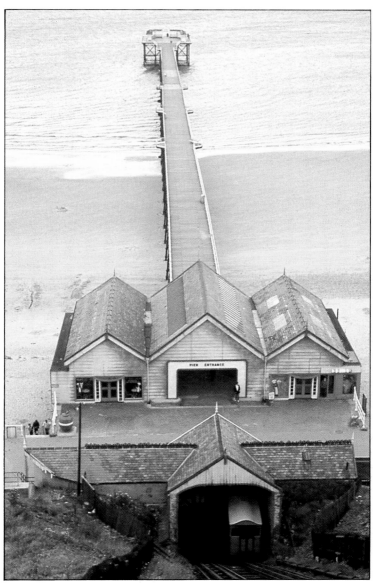

▲ Good architectural photography relies very heavily on the right light for the subject. In this shot of a pier in Yorkshire, strong sun would have given the roofs and their sharp shadows undue importance. As it is, slight gradations of tone and colour can be explored as the eye is carried downwards by the rush of the cable-car line and follows the slow expansion of the pier into the blue-grey sea. The red and blue trim of the sheds is softly repeated in the asphalt area between them and in the muted colours on the pier.

Use a Shift Lens

With a perspective control, or shift, lens on the camera, you can change the field of view by simply turning a knob. So instead of tilting the camera upwards, to include the top of a tall building for example, you can keep the camera level and avoid the problem of converging vertical lines.

● **Use a spirit level** to check that the camera back is precisely vertical. Tilting the camera will make parallel lines appear to converge.

● **Shift up** to bring the top of tall buildings into shot.

● **Shift down** to include more of the floor, or to photograph the top of a table without the legs converging towards the ground.

● **Shift sideways** in rooms with mirrors to avoid camera reflections appearing in the picture.

● **Do not shift too far,** or the corners of the picture will darken.

● **Fit a squared screen** to replace the normal focusing screen, and you will be able to verify that lines are parallel.

● **Stop down the lens** – when you are using small apertures you can shift the lens much farther.

● **Use the lens** to eliminate unwanted foreground, such as a street.

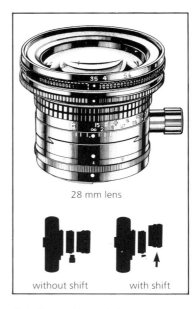

28 mm lens

without shift   with shift

▲ A 28mm wide-angle lens at ground level creates converging verticals (below left) as the camera has to be tilted. This can be corrected with a shift lens.

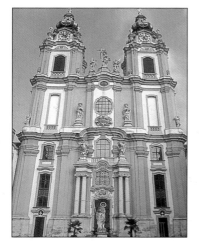

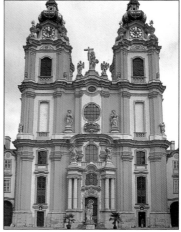

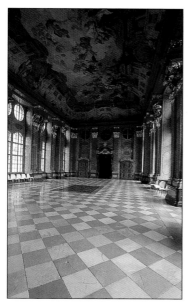

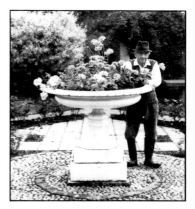

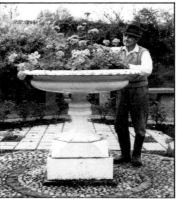

▲ For the interior, above, all I had available was a 35mm camera with a 28mm shift lens. By shifting the lens downwards a more intense feeling of the sheer volume of the space was captured. A shift lens, however, is not essential for successful architectural shots. In the example below, taken in New York, I moved well back from the group of buildings I wanted to shoot and used a telephoto lens aimed just above the street.

▲ The two photographs above illustrate how the background is apparently displaced without tilting the camera.

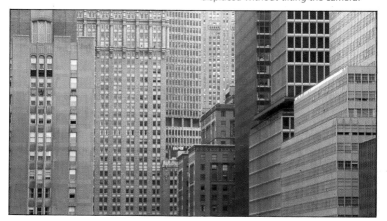

Make Rooms Look Bigger

Photographing a room to retain its essential features, and to create a sense of space, is not difficult, but does call for attention to detail. You need to select your viewpoint carefully, and you may need to rearrange the furniture so that it is not obtrusive.

● **Change lenses.** A standard lens is suitable only when you are taking pictures in an auditorium. A 28mm lens is the longest that really gives a sense of true space indoors; 20mm and 24mm lenses make rooms seem progressively bigger. Lenses of 18mm and shorter focal lengths introduce distortion.

● **Use a mirror.** Interior designers often place mirrors cleverly to make small rooms look bigger. Close to the camera, a mirror can be undetectable in a photograph; even if the frame is visible in the pitcture, the mirror will make the room will look larger than it really is.

● **Shoot through a door** or window. By backing out of the room you are photographing, you increase the camera-to-subject distance and with it the apparent space in the room.

● **Make use of shadows.** Place your main subject in a pool of light and take advantage of the dark surroundings. For all the viewer knows, that background may stretch away into the distance.

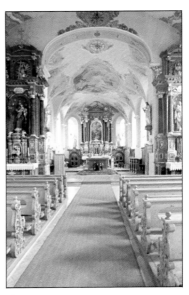

▲ For the church above: I used a 28mm lens, exposing for a second at *f*22, and a 16mm lens to increase the apparent size of the dining room (below).

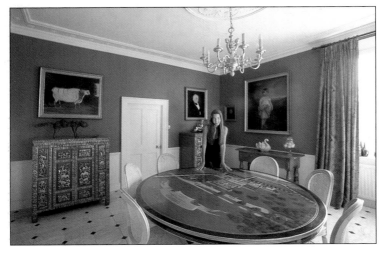

Photograph Dark Corners

To the eye, normal room lighting usually looks quite even, but if you take exposure readings from a point near the light source and from a dark corner, you will find that the most dimly lit part of a room is as much as six stops darker than a well-lit area. You can solve this in a number of ways.

● **Move your subject** into the light. If it is closer to a window, you may be able to hand-hold the camera.

● **Concentrate** on brightly lit areas. This is how I approached the problem of low light in the Buddhist shrine (right). It is not always essential that shadow areas of the picture retain full detail and in such situations you can take a reading from the highlights.

● **Use a reflector.** Placing a mirror just outside the frame is a quick way to double the amount of light falling on the subject. Even a newspaper reflects 80–90 per cent of the light falling on it.

● **Add some light.** In domestic interiors there are usually extra lamps available. Domestic tungsten lamps will create an orange colour cast, but this often makes the room look cosy. For perfect colour with ordinary 100W bulbs, use an 80A filter together with an 82B filter.

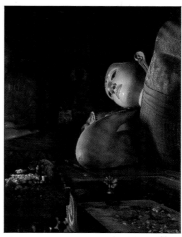

▲ Existing light was used to capture the bright colours and penetrating quiet of a Buddhist temple. I braced myself against a wall to shoot at 1/4 and *f*8.

▼ To photograph this woman working at her spinning wheel, I asked her to move into the area of light coming from the window.

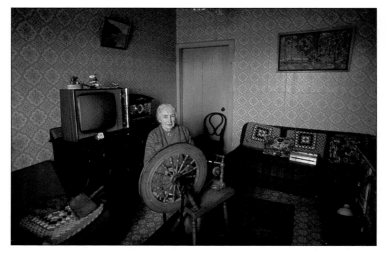

Feature Buildings

Our experience of architecture tends to be dynamic, not static. Walking around and through a building provides us with a constantly changing view that is impossible to capture in a single photograph. Try, therefore, to build up an impression of the structure through a series of images.

● **Think** before pressing the shutter release, and bear in mind that you are not trying to capture the picture that 'says it all' about the building. Rather, your aim is to build up a series of photographs that work together and convey a cumulative impression.

● **Look for details** that reveal more about the building than simply the overall view. These sorts of features are hard to discern in a long shot.

● **Be comprehensive.** It is always better to take too many photographs than too few. This will leave you with the option of editing out any unnecessary shots later on.

● **Make several visits** if time allows so that you can photograph aspects of the building in a range of different lights and varied weather.

● **Lay out your images** with care and attention to detail. Arrange them in such a way that the viewer's eye moves naturally from one picture to the next, just as you scanned the building.

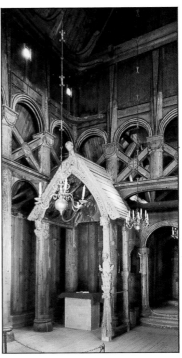

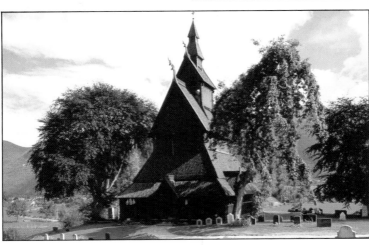

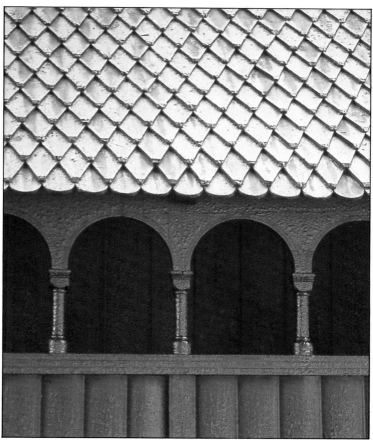

◀ Aspects of a Norwegian stave church build into a composite portrait of it. Opposite above is the canopied altar, which I took with four flashes from a small flash-gun. Below that is a sidelit exterior shot that brings out the contrast between the peaceful setting and the dark, sombre building. Above, I used a 100mm lens to flatten the perspective of the traditional wall made of upright staves, or planks, surmounted by arches. Light gives a sheen to the tarred planks and roof tiles, but the untarred wood on the sheltered wall glows warmly through. Finally, right, I used the same lens to get a close-up view of the dragons' heads that project from the gables like the prows of Viking longboats.

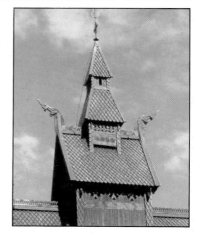

Paint with Flash

Large interiors are often too dark to photograph by available light, even with an exposure lasting many seconds. To solve the problem, a tecnhique called 'painting with light' has been developed. This consists of moving around the interior with a portable flash-gun, firing many small flashes. You need to practise, and to experiment with exposure, to get good results. It is better to underlight slightly than to overlight.

● **Fix the camera** on a tripod or place it on a ledge or table.

● **Set the shutter** to its B setting and use a locking cable release to hold the shutter open.

● **Set the flash** on 'manual' and pick an aperture that will render existing lights naturally in an exposure of about a minute. Use the aperture to give you your flash-to-subject distance. For example, the mosque below needed six flashes at about 3m (10ft).

● **Keep the flash** at a constant distance from the wall. With high ceilings, give extra flashes.

● **Avoid overlap.** Equally, make sure that there are no gaps.

● **Take several pictures** at different apertures to experiment.

● **Keep out of the picture** and wear dark clothing. If you stand between the camera and the flash, your silhouette will register.

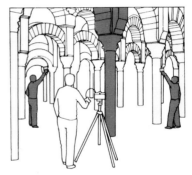

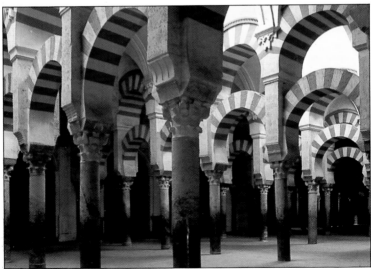

▲ Cordoba's Great Mosque was lit insufficiently, so I used six flashes during an exposure of one minute at *f*22.

▶ There were heavy shadows in the Gallery of Mirrors in the Palazzo Doria Pamphilj, Rome: I increased detail by adding 12 flashes at *f*32.

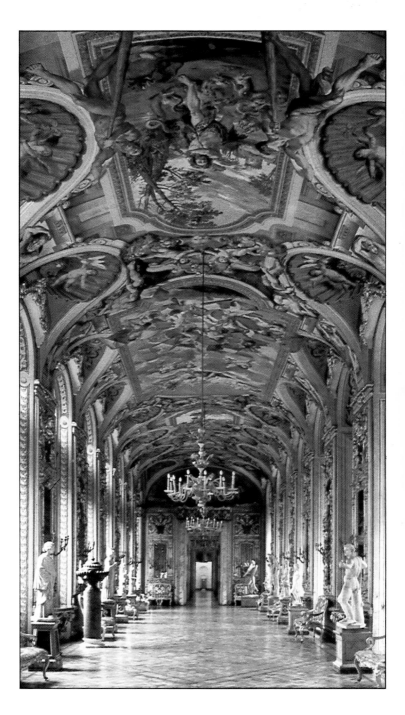

Avoid Stereotypes

Any place with a claim to fame has almost certainly been photographed a million times before and is almost certainly overrun with tourists. How do you capture the essential atmosphere of a place without ending up with a stereotype, and how do you clear the ground of all those milling hordes?

● **Rise early,** in order to miss the crowds that will clutter the scene later in the day.

● **Look** for the characteristics of the place that give it its unique quality and work out how you can express them in your photographs. For example, the mass of a huge reclining Buddha can be made more obvious if a child is included in the picture.

● **Find an unusual angle.** If you look hard enough, you will find one point from which you can work without people or litter being too obtrusive.

● **Find out** what the scene looks like from various angles. You should look at local postcards too: they are usually of the stereotyped views. Then search for an unusual viewpoint that will catch the scene differently.

● **Search for the detail** that epitomizes the whole. For example, it is almost impossible to find a time when a cathedral like St. Peter's in Rome is free of people, whether the devout or sightseers. So turn your camera to the aspects that illustrate the life of a great religious centre.

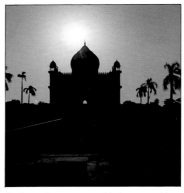

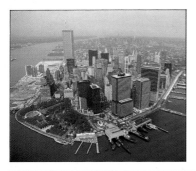

▲ The only way to avoid photographing litter in the pool leading to Akbar's tomb at Sikandra was to wait until sunset. Left, the usual shot of converging New York skyscrapers was avoided by taking a ride in a helicopter and (below) London's Tower Bridge was captured by using a telephoto lens just after sunset to capture the reflections of the lights in the Thames.

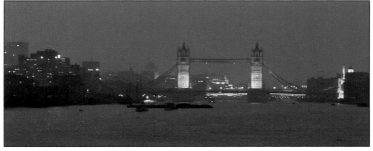

Shoot Through Glass

Unless you seek them to create an effect, reflections in glass are at best an irritating distraction and at worst can totally obscure the subject behind the glass. You can eliminate them by picking your lens and camera angle – and, where possible, the lighting – with care, and by using a polarizing filter.

● **Pick your angle** so that a dark subject is reflected in the glass – its weak reflections will not show up in the picture.

● **Pick your lighting** so that, if possible, the light on the far side of the glass, where your subject is, is brighter than on the camera side.

● **Use a polarizing filter.** This reduces reflections from most shiny surfaces. However, a polarizer works well only at certain angles to the surface. The best angle for glass is about 60°.

● **Rotate the filter** to determine the best orientation. All polarizers have rotating mounts and must be adjusted to the correct angle.

● **Choose a long lens,** which, with a polarizer, will kill reflections evenly across the frame. A wide-angle lens may not destroy them at the edges.

▶ Strong lighting inside the bakery helps reduce the effect of wet windows (top). A window frame can form a border to your picture (right). Car windows can be wound out of the way (below).

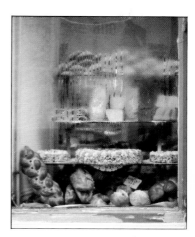

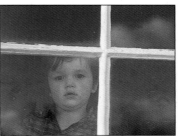

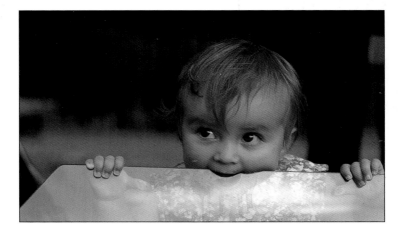

Use Reflections

Reflections can reveal new aspects of even familiar buildings, forcing the viewer to see them in a different way, and emphasizing features that might be buried by an overall impression of sheer bulk. Look for them in the glass of modern buildings, in mirrors, in stretches of water, and even in puddles.

● **Find well-lit subjects** and try to keep the reflecting surface in shadow, to maximize its reflective qualities. Mirrored glass reflects only when the light on the camera side is brighter than light on the other side. You will get the best results indoors at night and outdoors by day.

● **Pick oblique angles** when photographing reflections in plain glass or water. Head-on views do not give such bright reflections.

● **Throw stones** into still pools to break up reflections of the subject and thus make patterns more abstract.

● **Think small** and catch exciting reflections in small shiny surfaces, such as the hotel sign opposite.

● **Crop in tightly** using a telephoto lens to catch reflected glimpses of nearby buildings.

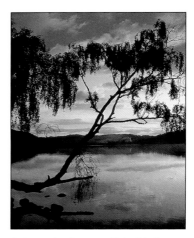

▲ A stretch of water will double the impact of a picture of the setting sun.

▼ Ripples in a glass façade distort the rigid lines of a modern block.

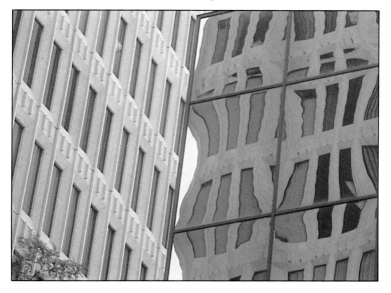

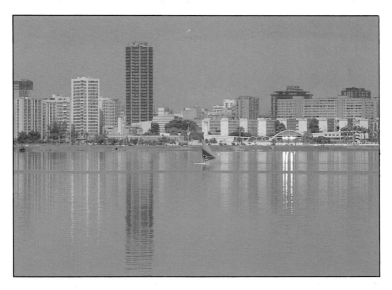

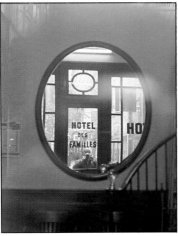

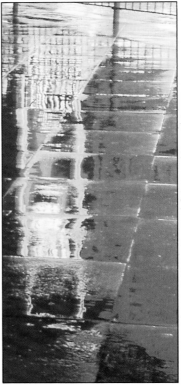

▲ Distant reflections of Rio de Janeiro create a delicate mirror image and a shimmering light.

▲ Shot through the glass door of a hotel, the picture above combines a sharply mirrored image with a softened interior and reflections from the street.

▶ A wet pavement makes an abstract pattern suggesting the colour and excitement of night in a big city.

Alter Hues

The camera never lies – but it may distort the truth a little, or present facts out of context. This final section of the book shows you how you can use a variety of effects and tricks to make things appear on film as they never did to the eye, beginning with a simple yet remarkably effective technique – that of changing the hues of a subject by using brightly coloured lights.

● **Buy a swatch** of coloured lighting gels from a theatrical lighting shop. Each gel in the swatch is small, but big enough to cover the reflector of a small flash unit. Tungsten lights will need larger squares of gel.

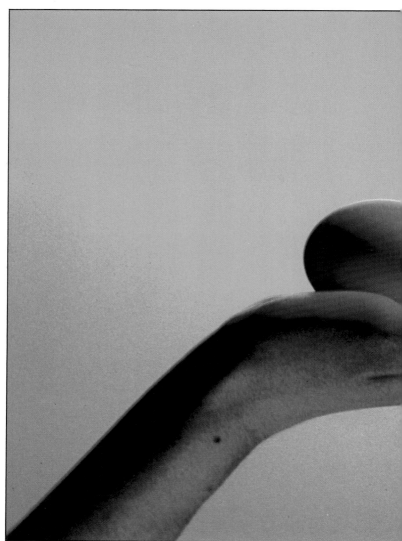

● **Pick strong colours** for the most dramatic effects: with weak colours the result may look like a mistake.

● **Leave space** for ventilation between the gel and the lamp.

● **Do not trust meters** or automatic flash-guns. Make exposure tests or bracket your pictures.

● **Experiment** by moving lights around and changing colours. Do not use too many colours. The best images are often very simple – like the one below.

▼ The egg and the girl's hand were lit by a red spotlight, and the white screen in the background by a blue light. The mixture of colours produced a white rim around the egg.

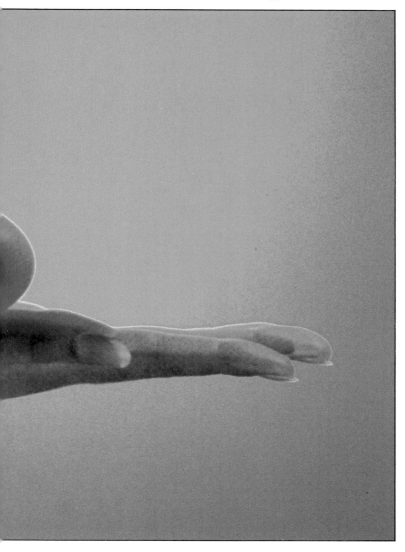

Use Filters for Fantasy

Filters are probably the cheapest of photographic accessories, yet they can have a greater impact on the appearance of your pictures than a special and expensive lens. Even if you expect to use special effects filters only rarely, it is worth tucking one or two into your camera bag just in case you are faced with a mundane or difficult subject.

● **Use special filters** with discretion or the effect will overpower your subject.

● **Use the preview button** to check the effect of the filter. With most it will vary according to the aperture.

● **Keep filters clean.** Dirt or scratches will cause flare. Also to avoid flare, never use more than two filters at once.

● **Use filter adapters** with lenses of different sizes.

▼ A dual colour filter was attached to create the picture of the wind turbines, while a slightly different dual colour filter was used for the view through the gnarled branches. An orange centre spot filter created the portrait effect. These filters come in a variety of colours.

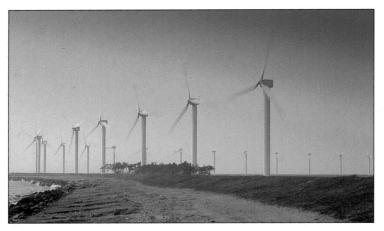

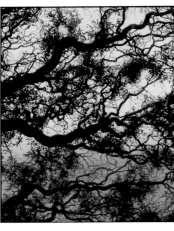

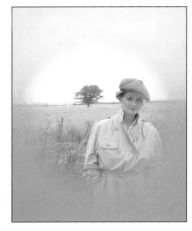

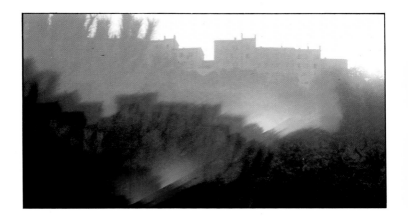

▲ Diffraction filters have ribbed surfaces that break light up into the spectrum. They can be used in combination with prism filters to deform the image. Prism filters repeat part of the image on separate facets of the lens attachment to suggest movement or to create patterns or surreal images.

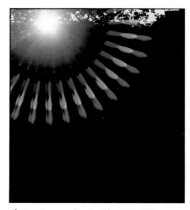

▲ Turning a wheel diffraction filter during exposure makes bands of colour.

▼ A triple colour filter was used to create this surreal, almost alien landscape. The incongruity of the orange and green clouds suggests a feeling of menace, which is enhanced by the dominant line of electricity pylons marching into the distance.

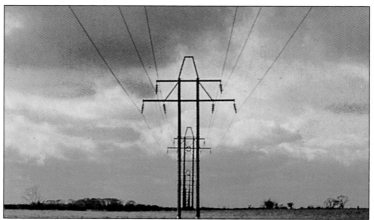

Colour Moving Objects

Colour film has three layers and so is sensitive to blue, green and red light. By filtering to expose the layers consecutively, rather than simultaneously, you can add brilliant colour to moving objects, while recording static ones in their natural hues.

● **Use negative film,** because colour balance is difficult to control using this technique. With negative film you can correct colour when printing.

● **Buy Wratten filters** as gelatin squares. Use numbers 25 (red), 61 (green) and 38A (blue).

● **Meter the scene** without the filters in place, then allow one extra stop for each exposure.

● **Make three exposures** on one frame, using a different coloured filter each time. See page 140 for details on multi-exposure techniques.

● **Choose subjects carefully.** Even static subjects can be coloured – provided that the sun is shining and that you allow half an hour or so between exposures. The shifting shadows then create delicate colour fringes.

▼ Red, green and blue filters, used successively in a triple exposure, gave normal colour in most of the picture, but recorded highlights of moving water in the inlet separately.

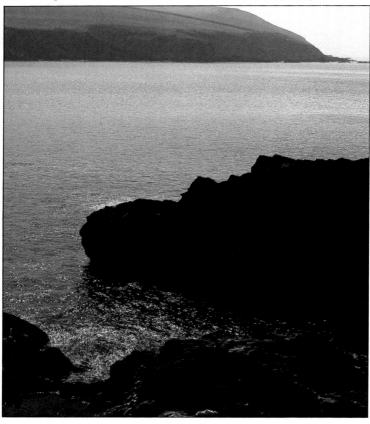

Add Highlight Sparkle

Starburst and diffraction filters spread highlights across the frame like brilliant bolts of lightning. With them you can make a rainswept, off-season seaside resort throb with energy and excitement or turn a string of paste into real diamonds.

● **Use starburst filters** – often called cross-screen filters – to make plain spikes of light. There is a range of filters, producing 2, 4, 6, 8 and 16 points from each highlight. The simplest filters usually produce the most successful pictures.

● **Use diffraction filters** to put colour into the picture, in addition to creating brilliant rays of light. Diffraction filters split white light into the colours of the spectrum, but have little effect on monochromatic light such as that from sodium streetlights.

● **Find a dark background,** so that the spikes stand out clear and bright.

● **Rotate the filter** during a long exposure to create a halo of light around each light source. With a diffraction filter this rotating action makes a rainbow effect.

● **Avoid fine detail,** because these filters will soften the picture and reduce the sharpness of the image.

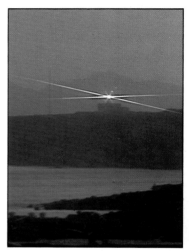

▲ A 'vario-starburst' diffraction filter made the lighthouse beam look more natural than if it had not been used.

▼ The repeating images created by a prism filter turn a city street at night into a blaze of colour.

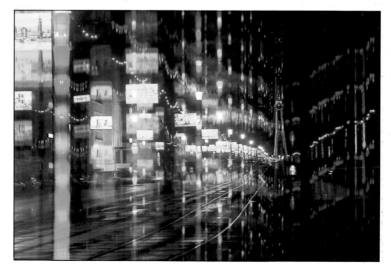

Keep Near and Far Sharp

There are occasions when you need to keep everything in a picture sharp, from something only a short distance from the camera to something that for all practical purposes is at infinity. Even a wide-angle lens stopped down to its smallest aperture may not give you the result you want. The answer is to fit a split-field close-up lens. This, sometimes called a half-lens, is literally that: a semicircle of magnifying glass which fits over your lens and brings near objects into focus while the main lens focuses farther back.

● **Base your choice** of lens on the distance of the foreground subject. A +1 lens focuses 1m (3ft) from the camera, and a +2 lens 0.5m (18in) away, etc.

● **Focus** for the distant subject and try to keep a featureless area in the centre of the picture, because the image blurs at the edge of the split field lens.

▼ A half-lens brought the foreground flowers into focus. Note the soft-focus boundary at the lens's edge half-way up the picture.

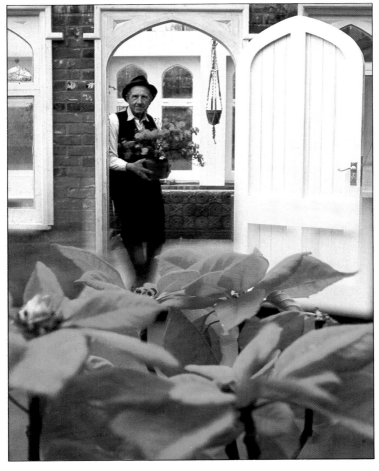

Compress Space

Extra-long telephoto lenses allow you to stand a long way from your subject, but have the effect of compressing space dramatically. Well-separated subjects appear to be on top of one another. To make the most of this characteristic, you need to understand long lenses and to choose subjects that exploit their qualities.

● **Use 200mm** or longer lenses. Shorter lengths do not produce a sufficiently pronounced effect.

● **Juxtapose** near and far in the same picture. If your subject stands alone, the compression will be less obvious.

● **Get similar subjects** into the same frame. Telephoto pictures look dramatic because they make the subjects look the same size in spite of the distance between them.

● **Shoot early in the day** or your picture will be veiled in haze.

▼ Long lenses reduce separation. Using a 400mm lens makes the church appear to be just in front of the mountains.

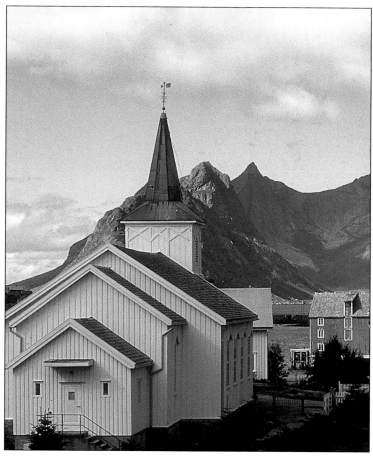

Exploit Wide Lenses

In many photographic applications, the faults and foibles of wide-angle lenses are a hindrance: no one wants converging verticals and bulging walls in a formal architectural picture. However, if your aim is to make an image that excites, rather than a picture that is geometrically and technically perfect, then it may be worthwhile to exaggerate the distortions that accompany wide-angle views.

● **Move close** to the subject to maximize distortion. A wide-angle lens permits you to fill the frame from a viewpoint near to the subject and, seen from such close proximity, perspective and size relationships are upset.

● **Tilt the camera** to make parallel lines coverage steeply as they recede into the distance. Patterned surfaces, such as as tiled walls or wooden floorboards, show the effect much more clearly than plain surfaces.

● **Frame off-centre.** Subjects at the corners and edges of the frame are distorted much more by wide-angle lenses than at the centre of the picture. Circular objects – such as footballs and faces – appear stretched dramatically in the corners of the picture.

● **Use fish-eye lenses** for the ultimate in distortion. Circular image fish-eyes make a round image on the film. Although such lenses produce striking images, the bubble shape is sometimes hard to accommodate on the printed page or on a wall of framed pictures. The full-frame fish-eye, which covers the whole of the 35mm format, is perhaps of practical use more often.

● **Save money** by using a wide-angle converter. This screws to the front of the lens and creates ultra-wide views. Another type turns a standard lens into a full-frame fish-eye and a 24mm lens into a circular image fish-eye.

▶ An 8mm fish-eye produced the picture opposite below, a 15mm wide-angle the distorted head opposite above. A more normal view – although still distorted – was obtained of the trumpeter by using a 24mm lens close to the instrument, with an aperture of f22.

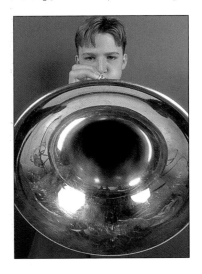

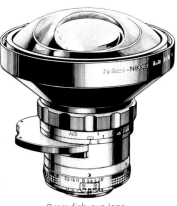

8mm fish-eye lens

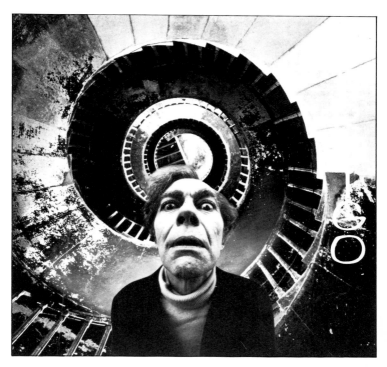

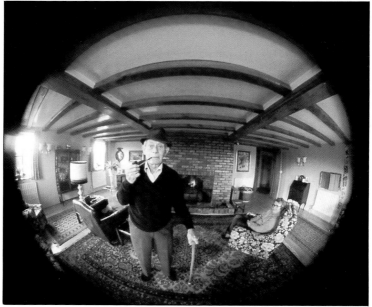

Find Exotic Backgrounds

Professional photographers often use projected backgrounds as substitutes for exotic real-life locations: palm-fringed islands can be created in the studio for a fraction of the cost of a trip to the Caribbean. Although professional front-projection equipment is sophisticated and expensive, you can simulate some of its effects with an ordinary slide projector.

● **Pick a slide** that gives an overall impression of the scene that you want as a background.

● **Match lighting** so that the light on the foreground figure is of the same quality, direction and intensity as the light on the background.

● **Avoid shadows appearing** on the background by keeping the subject well forward from the screen. This will also prevent subject-lighting falling onto the screen.

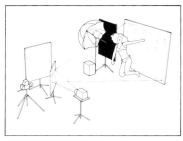

▲ I bounced the street scene off semi-transparent glass and aligned the camera so the model masked her shadow.

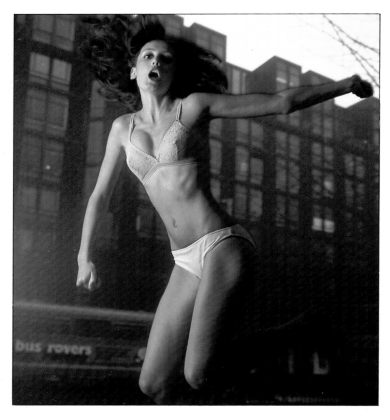

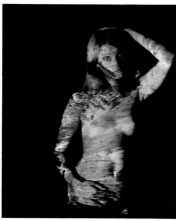

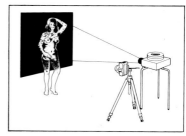

● **Match the colour** of foreground and background by shooting a test roll of film. Filter if necessary.

● **Use tungsten film** and floodlamps to match the projector's tungsten lamp.

● **Use angled glass** with the camera behind it for a true front-projection. Otherwise, try to keep the projector and camera as close together as possible.

● **Experiment** by projecting images onto your model.

▲ An abstract pattern projected onto the model produced this effect.

◀ I used a professional front-projection unit and studio lamps for this shot.

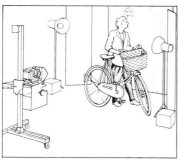

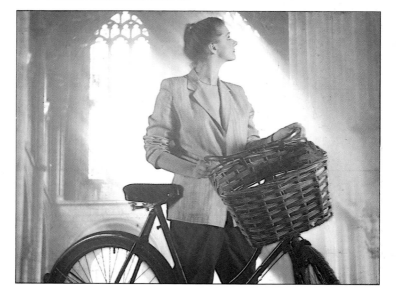

Mirror Images

A pool of water reflects light and colour like a mirror in constant motion. The slightest breeze or vibration changes the reflection, making a new, abstract pattern. This is particularly true of those modern building complexes in which a pool or a fountain reflects the geometric lines of today's design, but, when its surface is disturbed, gives them a gentler expression.

● **Explore different angles** and make use of brightly coloured subjects.

● **Use a zoom lens,** for instance 70–210mm, to select abstract areas.

● **Try using double exposure** to combine different reflections and straightforward shots.

● **Shatter the image** by blowing on the water's surface.

● **Use slower shutter speeds** to express the movement.

▼ A weathered boathouse, reflected in a river, gains the quality of tapestry from faint ripples.

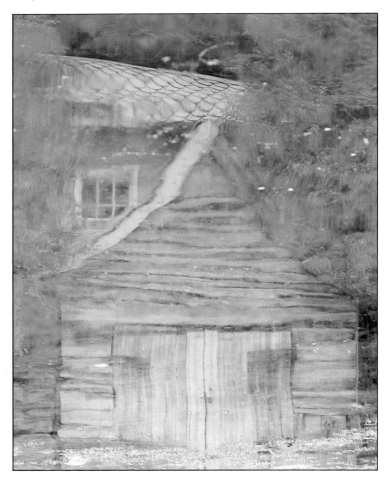

Create Distortions

The flowing, changing surface of a pool of water may add variety and randomness to your reflection photographs, but it is hardly conducive to repeatability. If you want to be more in control of the scene, you should look for a more permanent reflective medium. The materials available range from foil, which is cheap, to reflective acrylic sheet, which is not.

● **Pick reflectors** that have some rigidity of their own. Foil-covered card, tin sheets and reflective acrylic sheet can all be easily bent or flexed.

● **Stretch thin films** such as reflective acrylic sheet over timber frames. Heat the sheet before stapling it to the frame so that when it cools it becomes taut. Press it from behind to distort the normal reflection.

● **Use the viewfinder** to monitor progress as you build up the distorted image. From other angles the reflections will look quite different.

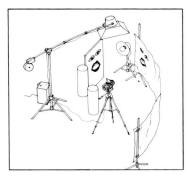

▲ Features stuck on a glazing sheet were distorted in a flexible plastic mirror and reflections added by foil cylinders.

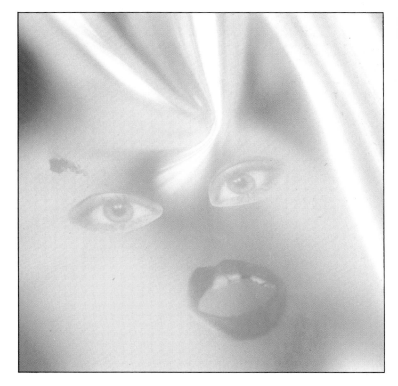

Use Infrared Film

Like ordinary colour film, infrared (IR) film has three layers, but because one of these layers is sensitive not to visible light but to infrared radiation, the film creates a bizarre world of distorted hues and brilliant colours. Foliage turns out brilliant pink and flesh tones an unearthly green.

● **Use a yellow filter,** because infrared colour film is sensitive to blue light, which creates a heavy colour cast on the pictures. A Kodak Wratten 12 filter is a good choice.

● **Put the film in the freezer** until you are about to use it. It is sensitive to heat, which will cause fogging.

● **Set your meter** to ISO 100 and take readings without the filter. Bracket exposures as your camera's TTL meter will not read the IR element in the light.

● **Focus normally** – the infrared focusing mark on your lens barrel is designed for use with black-and-white infrared film.

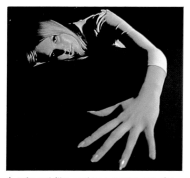

▲ Infrared film and two exposures, the second with a red filter, produced the bizarre portrait; the same film shot in natural light turned the foliage pink.

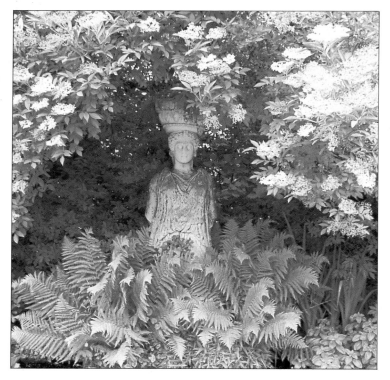

Make Hidden Supports

The camera sees the world around us from just one angle. By taking advantage of this limitation, you can produce trick photographs that confuse the viewer and demand attention. The knack in creating them lies in hiding the supporting structure.

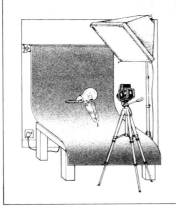

● **Pick subjects** that look unnatural when floating in air.

● **Suggest** that gravity has failed by supporting heavy subjects from below, against a plain background, and then shooting them from above. The viewer will automatically assume that the camera was horizontal.

● **Light carefully.** You must remember that light usually comes from above, that is, the top of the picture.

◀ A support soldered to the bulb's base, electric wires soldered to the terminals, and a pin through the feather created this illusion.

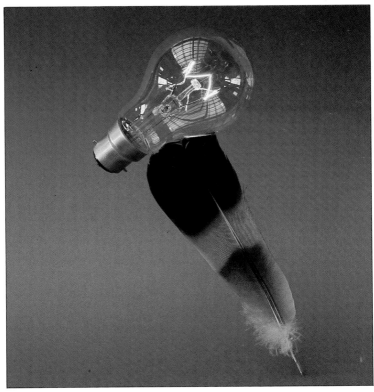

Double Expose

Multiple exposure is one of the most versatile of all special effects. Using it, you can combine several quite different picture elements within one frame.

● **Read your camera's instructions.** If it has a multi-exposure feature, double exposures easy. If it does not, follow these steps. You cannot double expose using cameras with auto wind-on.

● **Make the first exposure** – you may have to underexpose it, as I have mentioned below.

● **Tension the film** across the camera back by turning the film rewind knob until you have taken up all of the slack in the cassette. Then hold the crank firmly in place.

● **Press the rewind button,** which is usually on the camera's base plate.

● **Crank the lever wind.** This will tension the shutter without advancing the film to the next frame.

● **Make** the second exposure, possibly underexposing as before.

● **Cut the exposure time** when laying a larger image on top of a smaller one. For two images cut by one stop; for four, cut by two stops; for eight, cut by three stops; and so on.

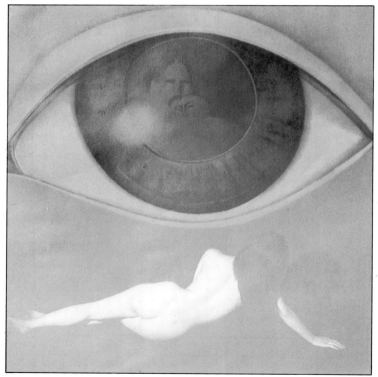

▲ The eye was cut from a magazine. I photographed it with a Hasselblad, marking the position of the bottom of the eyelid on the camera screen and underexposing by half a stop. Then, with the girl against a black backdrop, I positioned her in the lower half of the viewfinder and re-exposed the frame.

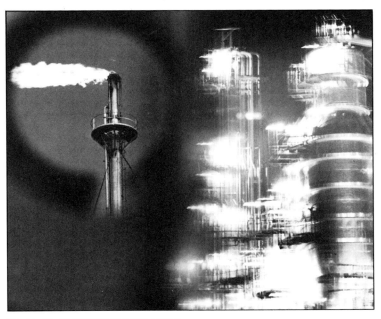

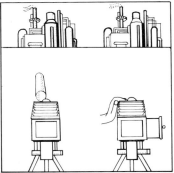

▼ I took the girl, who was in black clothes against a black backdrop, through a double-exposure filter and then rotated the filter 180° to add her hands and feet.

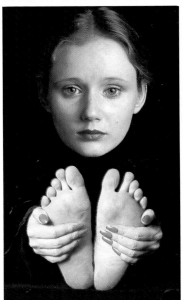

▲ To make this picture I used a plate camera, which let me double-expose one half of the negative while giving the other half only one exposure. The jet of flame is seen through a tube of rolled metal foil, held in front of the one side of the lens. The first exposure thus recorded both the refinery and the flame. During the second exposure, I slid the sheath across half the frame to cover the jet and gently tapped the tripod so that vibration produced a double-exposed image of the refinery that seems to quiver with power.

Combine Images on Slide

Multiple exposure is not the only way to combine images: you can also sandwich together slides or negatives to overlay one frame on another. This technique has the advantage that you can produce multiple images from your existing file of photographs.

● **Pick thin slides,** because the process of sandwiching is additive: if you combine pictures of normal density the resulting sandwich will be too dark.

● **Clean each slide** very thoroughly. Remember that you are doubling the number of surfaces on which the dust and dirt can collect.

● **Align the images** on a lightbox. If you do not have one, tape a piece of tracing paper to a window and use this to illuminate the slides from behind. Alternatively, put a table lamp under a glass surface such as a coffee table.

● **Tape the frames** together so that they cannot move out of alignment. Slide mounts alone will not keep pictures in register.

▼ To check if slides are suitable for combining, remove them from their mounts, tape them together, remount them and then project them. The two slides combined in the shot below were shot specially. The background remained exactly the same for each shot (the camera was mounted on a tripod), but the model moved and was lit each time with a differently coloured filter over the flash.

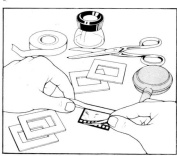

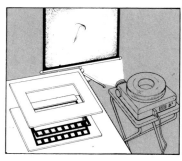

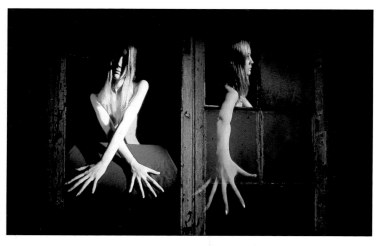

Multiply the Image

A multi-image prism is a quick and convenient way to inject movement into static or lacklustre subjects. The lens screws into the front of your main lens just like a filter and its faceted surface splits the subject into several identical images.

● **Pick dark backgrounds** and bright subjects so the images that surround the main subject will stand out clearly.

● **Use different lenses** to alter the spacing of multiple images on the frame.

● **Stop down the lens,** as these prisms can reduce contrast and definition in the final result.

● **Shade the lens** from direct light, as the extra glass surface can cause flare. Make sure, though, that the shading does not appear in the picture.

● **Colour the facets** of the prism with a felt-tipped pen. This will colour the individual images.

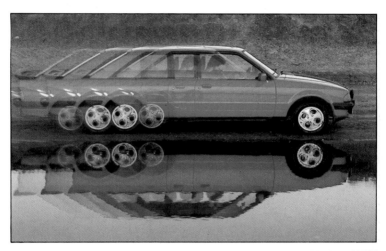

▲ A four-band prism lens added an impression of movement to a parked car; three-band lenses added interest to the former County Hall in London (right). A variety of prism lenses is available that enable the photographer to repeat an image in a number of patterns.

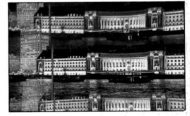

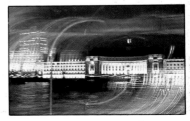

Copy Images

Copying photographs is a straightforward, almost mechanical process, yet it has a fundamental importance in many special effects techniques. For example, when you have created a photomontage from several images, you can copy the result to make a seamless print. The technique can be used to copy paintings, drawn artwork, and even solid objects like badges.

● **Use a tripod** and cable release to hold the camera steady. Alternatively, for small subjects, use a copy stand.

● **Make the lighting even** by arranging a lamp on either side of the subject to be copied. Even two small electronic flash units will do, although tungsten lamps are easier to use. Check lighting balance by measuring the distance from each lamp to the middle of the subject or by standing a pencil up in the centre of the subject – the shadows on each side should be equally dark and of the same length.

● **Load slow film,** with an ISO rating of between 25–100.

● **Eliminate reflections,** both of the lights and the camera, or they will appear in the picture. Cover the camera with black velvet – cut a hole for the lens. Reflections of the lights can usually be eliminated by repositioning them on either side of the subject being copied.

● **Set exposure** by covering the subject with a Kodak Neutral Gray card, then use your TTL meter. This prevents subject tones from influencing the reading. As a makeshift alternative, take a reading from the dull side of a sheet of brown wrapping paper. Bracket exposures to be sure of good results.

● **Use a standard** or a macro lens. These will give sharper pictures than lenses of other focal lengths. Stop the lens down to *f*8 or a smaller aperture.

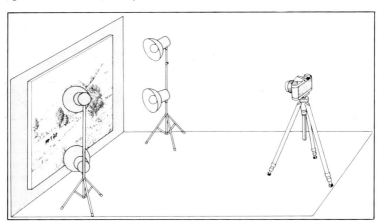

▲ To light a large subject evenly, use four lamps, aiming each at a corner of the subject. They should be placed between 1–2m (about 3–6ft) from the subject and at an angle of about 45° to its surface. The camera should be placed some distance away in order to avoid flare.

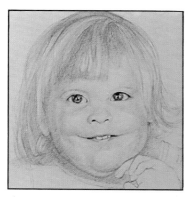

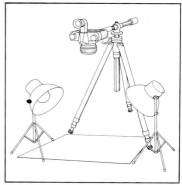

▲ To copy drawings and engravings, use a cross-arm tripod (above right). To check alignment, put a mirror flat on the original and adjust the camera until a reflection of the lens is in the centre of the viewfinder. If you are working with tungsten lamps, angle them down at 45°. For engravings or drawings, use line or lith film. For continuous-tone originals, use slow, normal-contrast film.

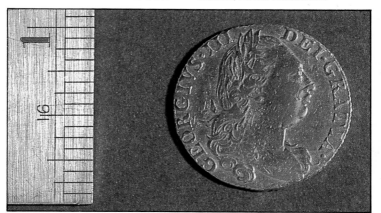

▲ Photograph a coin by placing it on a contrasting or black background and position the camera above using a tripod or copying stand. To bring out the relief, illuminate it with a spotlight placed a metre (3ft) or so away and pointing down at about 30° to the copyboard. Fit a lens hood to eliminate flare or reflections. To bring out surface detail, you will need to use front or oblique lighting. This can be obtained with a ring flash or a glass sheet and a spotlight. Use a clamp to fix the glass at 45° between the camera and the subject. Place the light about a metre (3ft) away.

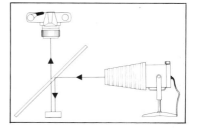

Control Tones

Coloured filters have special value when used with black-and-white film. They lighten those parts of the subject that are the same colour as the filter, and darken complementary colours. So, by picking your filter, you can control precisely the tones that, in a black-and-white print, represent the colours of the spectrum.

● **Use an ultraviolet** filter to cut down haze and to protect the lens.

● **Use yellow filters** to darken blue sky slightly, to render the tones of stone, fabric and sand accurately, and to lighten foliage a little.

● **Use orange filters** to produce more pronounced effects than can be achieved with yellow filters.

● **Use red filters** for really dramatic effects – blue sky becomes almost black.

● **Use blue filters** to exaggerate the effects of haze and mist.

● **Filter portraits** to control skin tones. A red filter will hide skin blemishes; a green one will make a pale-skinned person look weather-beaten and healthy. A yellow filter is useful indoors.

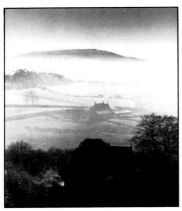
▲ Ultraviolet filters cut haze.

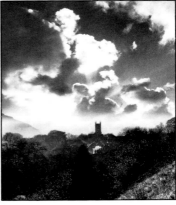
▲ Red filters darken skies.

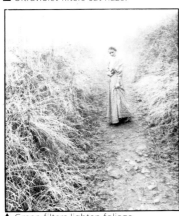
▲ Green filters lighten foliage.

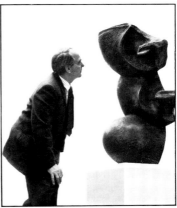
▲ Yellow filters give natural tones.

Exaggerate Grain

Photographers usually regard grain as a bugbear – something to avoid at all costs. This need not be the case. You can use the effects of grain creatively, to give your prints a pronounced surface texture or to suggest an atmosphere of gritty realism.

● **Make grain prominent** in the following ways:

● **Use fast film,** which has large grain. Kodak Tri-X is a good choice for this.

● **Overexpose the film** a little. Rate Tri-X at ISO 800 instead of its normal ISO 400.

● **Overdevelop the film** by leaving it in the developer for twice as long as usual. Continuous agitation can help.

● **Make big enlargements** from part of the negative. Print on glossy paper in a hard grade to get extra contrast.

▼ Accentuated grain enhances the appeal of this picture.

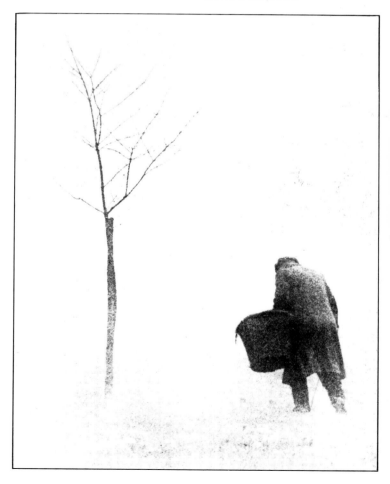

Make Photo Montages

The cut-and-paste simplicity of photomontage may seem primitive when compared to the effects possible with a modern personal computer with suitable image manipulation software, but the manual approach can show you what is possible with a limited budget and patience.

● **Use imagination** in choosing suitable combinations of subjects. Do not be bound by convention: the most surreal and bizarre juxtapositions are often the most exciting.

● **Match prints** for density, contrast and lighting or the joins will be obvious.

● **Plan** where you want each element to fall, using a sheet of tracing paper.

● **Cut the pictures** two-thirds through from the back, then tear them: the

result is a ready-bevelled edge that pastes down easily and evenly.

● **Bevel the cut edges** of the pictures with very fine sandpaper so that the images blend smoothly.

● **Paste the picture down** onto a stout piece of cardboard using rubber cement. Make sure that no glue remains around the joins.

● **Rephotograph the image** for best results (see page 144).

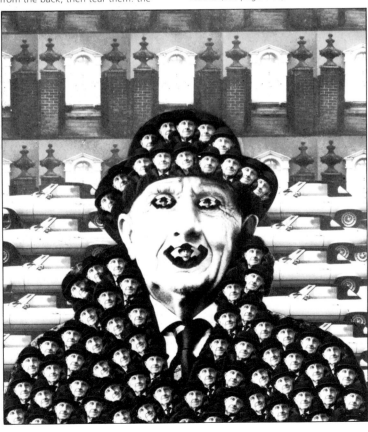

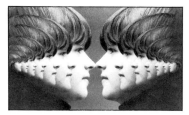

▲ Seven straight prints and then seven more with the negative reversed produced this portrait.

◀ The montage of the man in the bowler hat opposite required 160 separate printings of the same image. The car and the architectural features also had to be printed the required number of times. All the images were mounted and reshot.

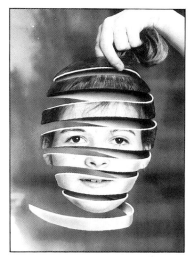

▼ A life-sized print of a section of the sphere, glued to the fork, and a piece of black card, glued to the sphere, are the keys to this montage.

▲ To make this portrait, I cut a portrait up into strips and then glued them onto a tin spiral. I then rephotographed the result with a hand holding the spiral.

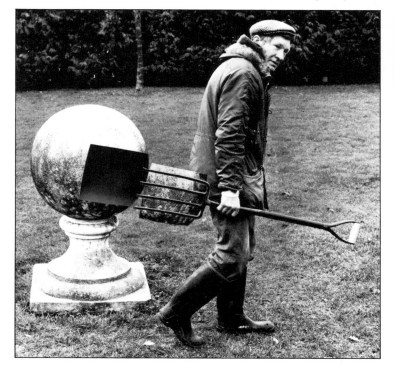

Take Pictures off TV

Television provides a virtually limitless number of marvellous images, each subtly different from its predecessor and its successor. On location in your living room, you can make a permanent record of the history of our times. Remember, though, that television is protected by copyright laws.

● **Use a tripod** to lock your camera rigidly in position in front of the centre of the screen.

● **Cut the colour intensity** of the image on the screen to a little lower than normal.

● **Draw the curtains** and turn out the room lights to eliminate reflections.

● **Take a meter reading** close to the screen or use automatic.

● **Set the shutter** to 1/15 or slower to enable each picture scan to be completed: faster speeds will record a dark band across the image.

● **Use your video recorder** to freeze-frame fast moving action and photograph the still image.

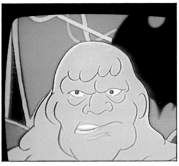

▲ TV provides almost every kind of image. If you are using daylight colour film, try fitting a Kodak CC40R filter to cut any blue-green cast, or, alternatively, make the colour on the set a little redder. You will find that simple images, such as the cartoon above, offer scope for later montage work.

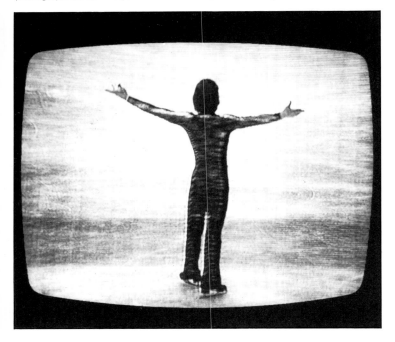

Photograph Scale Models

In the film industry elaborate scale models are used to reconstruct history, envisage the future, or save costs. Model-making at that level is a highly skilled craft, but by adapting some of the movie-makers' tricks and techniques, you can create similar effects on top of a kitchen table.

● **Make a reduced scale model** with photography in mind. Since the camera sees only one side of a model, you need only build one side. The detail can be cruder if the camera is going to be some distance away.

● **Build background** in scale. Sand is too coarse in close-up – use Fuller's earth, flour or cement to simulate earth. Stars can be put in behind space models by pricking holes in a sheet of black card and backlighting it.

● **Arrange the lighting** to look as realistic as possible. Use a flash-gun from a distance to stimulate the sun.

● **Pick the viewpoint carefully.** The camera needs to be at 'ground level' and usually close to the subject. Use a wide-angle lens and stop down as far as you possibly can.

● **Create aerial perspective** by blowing smoke across the scene.

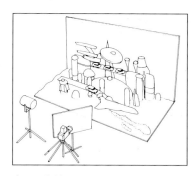

▲ Careful but inexpensive model-making lay behind the futuristic still life composition below. In order to light the scene evenly, I shot the set-up through a semi-silvered mirror angled at 45° in front of the camera. I then reflected a light off the mirror to create the impression of frontal lighting.

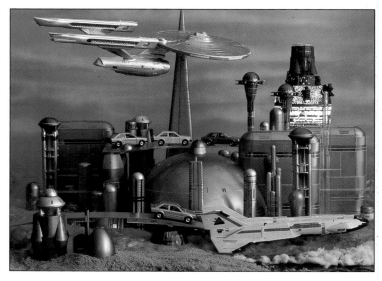

Glossary

Words shown in capitals indicate cross references within the glossary.

A

Aberration. Inherent fault in a lens image. Aberrations include ASTIGMATISM, BARREL DISTORTION, CHROMATIC ABERRATION, COMA, SPHERICAL ABERRATION. COMPOUND LENSES minimize aberrations.

Actinic. Describes light that is able to affect photographic material. With ordinary film, visible light and some ultraviolet light is actinic, while infrared light is not.

Acutance. Objective measure of image sharpness.

Airbrush. An instrument used by photographers for retouching prints. It uses a controlled flow of compressed air to spray paint or dye.

Air release. An extended CABLE RELEASE that uses pneumatic pressure to release the SHUTTER, operated by means of a small air bulb.

Anamorphic lens. Special lens that compresses the image in one dimension by means of cylindrical or prismatic elements. The image can be restored to normal after photography by using a similar lens for printing or projection.

Angle of view. Strictly, the angle subtended by the diagonal of the film format at the rear NODAL POINT of the lens. Generally taken to mean the wider angle 'seen' by a given lens. The longer the focal length of a lens, the narrower its angle of view. See also COVERING POWER.

Aperture. Strictly, the opening that limits the amount of light reaching the film and hence the brightness of the image. In some cameras the aperture is of a fixed size; in others it is in the form of an opening in a barrier called the DIAPHRAGM and can be varied in size. (An iris diaphragm forms a continuously variable opening, while a stop plate has a number of holes of varying sizes). Photographers, however, generally use the term 'aperture' to refer to the size of this opening. See also F NUMBER.

ASA. American Standards Association, which devised one of the two early systems for rating the SPEED of an EMULSION. See also DIN and ISO.

Astigmatism. The inability of a lens to focus vertical and horizontal lines in the same FOCAL PLANE. Corrected lenses are called 'anastigmatic'.

Automatic camera. Camera in which the exposure is selected automatically. A semi-automatic camera requires the user to pre-select the shutter speed or the aperture.

B

Back projection. The projection of slides onto a translucent screen from behind, instead of onto the front of a reflective screen.

Ball-and-socket head. A type of tripod fitting that allows the camera to be secured at the required angle by fastening a single locking screw. See also PAN-AND-TILT HEAD.

Barn doors. Hinged flaps for studio lamps, used to control the beam of light.

Barrel distortion. Lens defect characterized by the distortion of straight lines at the edges of an image so that they curve inward at the corners of the frame.

Bas relief. The special effect created when a negative and positive are sandwiched together and printed slightly out of register. The resulting picture gives the impression of being carved in low relief, like a bas-relief sculpture.

Beaded screen. Type of front-projection screen. The surface is covered with minute glass beads, giving a brighter picture than a plain white screen.

Bellows. Light-tight folding bag made of pleated material used to join the lens to the camera body. Found on large studio cameras, and used as an accessory for close-up work with smaller formats.

Between-the-lens shutter. One of two main types of shutter. Situated close to the DIAPHRAGM, it consists of thin metal blades or leaves that spring open and then close when the camera is fired, exposing the film. See also FOCAL-PLANE SHUTTER.

Bloom. Thin coating of metallic fluoride on the air-glass surface of a lens. It reduces reflections at that surface.

Bounced flash. Soft light achieved by aiming flash at a wall or ceiling to avoid the harsh shadows that result if the light is pointed directly at the subject. Tungsten light can be bounced in the same way.

Bracketing. Technique for ensuring the correct EXPOSURE by taking several photographs of the same subject at slightly different exposure settings. The bracketed sequence is usually taken with exposures at regular STOP intervals.

B setting. Setting on the shutter speed dial of a camera at which the SHUTTER remains open for as long as the release button is held down, allowing longer EXPOSURES than the preset speeds on the camera. The 'B' stands for 'bulb' for historical reasons. See also T SETTING.

BSI. British Standards Institution, which has an independent system of rating emulsion speed, similar to the ASA system. However, the BSI system is used as an industrial standard.

Bulk loader. Device for handling film that has been bought in bulk in a single length and which needs to be cut and loaded into cassettes.

C

Cable release. Simple camera accessory used to reduce camera vibrations when the shutter is released on a camera that is supported on a tripod, particularly when a relatively long EXPOSURE is being used.

Camera movements. Adjustments to the relative positions of the lens and the film whereby the geometry of the image can be controlled. A full range of movements is a particular feature of large-format cameras, although a few smaller cameras allow limited movements, and special lenses are available that do a similar job for 35mm SLRs.

Camera obscura. Literally a 'dark chamber'. An optical system, adopted before the advent of photography, using a pinhole or a lens to project an image onto a screen. One form of camera obscura, designed as an artist's aid, is the ancestor of the modern camera.

Canada balsam. Resin used to cement together pieces of optical glass, such as elements of a lens. When set it has a refractive index almost exactly equal to that of glass.

Cartridge. Plastic container of film such as the old 126 or 110 formats. The film is wound inside the cartridge from one spool onto a second spool.

Cassette. Container for 35mm or APS film. After EXPOSURE the film is wound back onto the cassette spool before the camera is opened.

Cast. Overall shift towards a particular hue, giving colour photographs an unnatural appearance.

CdS cell. Photosensitive cell used in some light meters, incorporating a cadmium sulphide resistor, which regulates electric current.

Centre-weighted meter. Type of TTL METER. The reading is most strongly influenced by the intensity of light at the centre of the image.

Chromatic aberration. The inability of a lens to focus different colours on the same focal plane.

Circle of confusion. Disc of light on the image produced by a lens when a point on the subject is not perfectly brought into focus. When looking at a photograph, the eye cannot distinguish between a very small circle of confusion (with a diameter of less than about 0.25mm/⅟₁₀₀in) and a true point.

Close-up lens. Simple positive lens placed over the normal lens to magnify the image. The strength of the close-up lens is measured in diopters.

Colour conversion filters. Camera filters required when daylight colour film is used in artificial light, or when film balanced for artificial light is used in daylight.

Colour correction filters. Filters used to correct slight irregularities in colour caused by specific light sources. Also refers to the cyan, magenta and yellow filters that are used to balance the colour of prints made from colour negatives.

Colour negative film. Film giving colour negatives, intended for printing.

Colour reversal film. Film giving colour positives (called slides or transparencies). Prints can also be made directly from these positives using special paper and chemicals.

Colour temperature. Measure of the relative blueness or redness of a light source, expressed in KELVIN. The human eye adjusts to differences in colour temperature automatically most of the time, but colour film is balanced to work with a single colour temperature – usually average daylight, or tungsten bulb lighting.

Coma. A lens defect that results in off-axis points of light appearing in the image not as points but as discs with comet-like tails.

Compound lens. Lens consisting of more than one element, designed so that the faults of the various elements largely cancel each other out.

Condenser. Optical system consisting of one or two plano-convex lenses (flat on one side, curving outward on the other) used in an enlarger or slide projector to concentrate light from a source and focus it on the negative or slide.

Contact print. Print that is the same size as the negative, made by sandwiching together the negative and the photographic paper when making the print. A whole roll of 35mm film can be contact printed at once onto one sheet of 25.4 x 20.3cm (10 x 8in) paper.

Converging lens. Any lens that is thicker in the middle than at the edges. Such lenses are able to cause parallel light to converge onto a point of focus, giving an image. Also known as a positive lens.

Converging verticals. Distorted appearance of vertical lines in an image, produced when the camera is tilted upwards. Tall objects such as buildings, for instance, appear to be leaning backward. Can be partially corrected at the printing stage, or by the use of CAMERA MOVEMENTS.

Converter. Auxiliary lens, usually fitted between the camera body and the principal lens, giving a combined FOCAL LENGTH that is greater than that of the principal lens alone. Most converters increase focal length by a factor of two or three. Also known as teleconverters.

Convertible lens. Compound lens consisting of two lens assemblies used separately or together. The two sections are usually of differing focal lengths, giving three possible permutations.

Correction filters. Colour filters used over the camera lens to modify the tonal balance of black and white images. See COLOUR CORRECTION FILTERS.

Covering power. The largest image area of acceptable quality that a given lens produces. The covering power of a lens is usually only slightly greater than the standard negative size for which it is intended. However, in a lens designed for use with a camera with movements (see CAMERA MOVEMENTS), the covering power must be considerably greater.

Cropping. Enlarging only a selected portion of the negative instead of printing the entire area.

D

Daylight film. Colour film balanced to give accurate colour rendering in average daylight, that is to say, when the COLOUR TEMPERATURE of the light source is around 5500 Kelvin. Also suitable for use with electronic flash.

Density. The light-absorbing power of a photographic image. A logarithmic scale is used in measurements: 50 per cent absorption is expressed as 0.3, 100 per cent is expressed as 1.0, etc. In general terms, density is simply the opaqueness of a negative or the blackness of a print.

Depth of field. Zone of acceptable sharpness extending in front of and behind the plane of the subject that is exactly focused by the lens.

Depth of focus. Very narrow zone behind the lens within which slight variation in the position of the film makes no appreciable difference to the focusing of the image.

Diaphragm. System of adjustable metal blades forming a roughly circular opening of variable diameter, used to control the APERTURE of a lens.

Diapositive. Alternative name for TRANSPARENCY.

Differential focusing. Technique involving the use of shallow depth of field to enhance the illusion of depth and solidity in a photograph.

Diffraction. Phenomenon occurring when light passes close to the edge of an opaque body or through a narrow APERTURE. The light is slightly deflected, setting up interference patterns that may sometimes be seen as fuzziness. The effect is occasionally noticeable in photography, when, for example, a very small lens aperture is used.

DIN. Deutsche Industrie Norm, the German standards association that devised one of the old systems used for rating the speed of an EMULSION. On the DIN scale, every increase of 3 indicates that the sensitivity of the emulsion has doubled. See also ASA and ISO.

Diverging lens. Any lens that is thicker at the edges than in the middle. Such lenses cause parallel rays of light to diverge, forming an image on the same side of the lens as the subject. Diverging lenses are also known as negative lenses.

D-max. Technical term for the maximum DENSITY of which a given type of EMULSION is capable.

E

Electronic flash. Type of flash-gun that uses the brief flash of light produced by a high-voltage electrical discharge between two electrodes in a gas-filled tube.

Emulsion. In photography, the light-sensitive layer or layers of a photographic material.

Exposure. The total amount of light allowed to reach the light-sensitive material during the formation of the LATENT IMAGE. The exposure is dependent on the brightness of the image, the camera APERTURE, and on the length of time for which the photographic material is exposed.

Exposure meter. Instrument for measuring the intensity of light so as to determine the correct SHUTTER and APERTURE settings.

Extension tubes. Accessories used in close-up photography, consisting of metal tubes that can be fitted between the lens and camera body, thus increasing the lens-to-film distance.

F

Fast lens. Lens with a wide maximum APERTURE, relative to its FOCAL LENGTH.

Fill-in. Additional lighting used to supplement the principal light source and to brighten shadows.

Film speed. The sensitivity of a film to light, usually expressed as a rating on the ISO scale.

Filter. Transparent sheet usually made of glass or plastic that is used to block a specific part of the light passing through it or to change or distort the image in some way. See also COLOUR CONVERSION FILTERS, COLOUR CORRECTION FILTERS, CORRECTION FILTERS and POLARIZING FILTERS.

Filter pack. Assembly of filters used in an enlarger when making colour prints. Normally consists of any two of the three subtractive primaries (yellow, magenta, cyan) in the appropriate strengths.

Fish-eye lens. Extreme wide-angle lens, with an ANGLE OF VIEW of about 180°.

Fixed-focus lens. Lens permanently focused at a fixed distance. Most cheap cameras use this system, giving sharp pictures from about 2 m (6ft) to infinity.

Flare. Unwanted light reflected inside the camera or between the elements of the lens giving rise to irregular marks on the negative and degrading the quality of the image. This can be overcome to some extent by using a lens coating, or a LENS HOOD.

Flashbulb. Expendable bulb with a filament of metal foil which is designed to burn up very rapidly giving a brief, intense flare of light, sufficiently bright to allow a photograph to be taken. Most flashbulbs have a light blue plastic coating, which gives the flash a COLOUR TEMPERATURE close to that of daylight.

Flashing. Photographic technique involving deliberately fogging a print briefly with white light during exposure. The effect is to control contrast. The extra exposure may be spread equally over the whole print, producing a soft overall effect; it may be used for vignetting so that the image merges into a black border, or it may be directed to a particular area by means of a torch to cause local darkening.

Floodlight. A general term for an artificial light source that provides a constant and continuous output of light suitable for studio photography or similar work. Usually consists of a 200–500 watt tungsten-filament bulb that is mounted in a REFLECTOR.

F number. Aperture setting. The number refers to the focal length of the lens divided by the diameter of the APERTURE. Because f numbers are RECIPROCALS, the bigger the number the smaller the aperture – thus f32 is smaller than f8. The f numbers available with a particular lens and camera generally follow a standard sequence, in which the interval between one STOP and the next represents a halving or doubling in the image brightness.

Focal length. Distance between the optical centre of the lens and the point at which rays of light parallel to the optical axis are brought to a focus. In general, the greater the focal length of a lens, the smaller its ANGLE OF VIEW.

Focal plane. Plane on which a given subject is brought to a sharp focus, which is the same as the plane on which the film is positioned.

Focal-plane shutter. One of the main types of SHUTTER, used almost universally in SINGLE-LENS REFLEX cameras. Positioned behind the lens (but slightly in front of the FOCAL PLANE), the shutter consists of a system of blinds or blades. When the camera is fired, a slit travels across the image area either vertically or horizontally. The width and the speed of travel of the slit determine the duration of the EXPOSURE. See also BETWEEN-THE-LENS SHUTTER.

Fog. Veiling of an image caused by accidentally exposing the film or paper; by overactive developer or weak fixer containing heavy deposits of silver salts; by overlong storage; or by exposure to powerful X-rays.

Forced development. Technique used to increase the effective speed of a film by extending its normal development time. Also known as PUSHING the film.

Format. Dimensions of the image recorded on the film by a given type of camera.

Fresnel lens. Lens whose surface consists of a series of concentric circular 'steps', each of which is shaped like part of the surface of a convex lens. Fresnel lenses are often used in the focusing screens of cameras to help improve the brightness of the image seen through the viewfinder. They are also used in spotlights to concentrate the light beam.

G

Gelatin. Material used as a binding for the EMULSION of photographic paper and film.

Glazing. Process by which glossy prints can be given a shiny finish by being dried in contact with a hot drum or plate of chromium or steel.

Grain. Granular texture appearing to some degree in all processed photographic materials. In black and white photographs the grains are clumps of particles of black metallic silver that constitute the dark areas of a photograph. In colour photographs the silver has been removed chemically but tiny blotches of dye retain the appearance of graininess. The faster the film the coarser the texture of the grain.

Granularity. Objective measure of graininess.

Guide number. Number indicating the effective power of a flash unit. For a given FILM SPEED, the guide number

divided by the distance between the flash and the subject gives the appropriate F NUMBER to use.

H

Halation. Phenomenon characterized by a halo-like band around the developed image of a bright light source. It is caused by internal reflection of light from the support of the EMULSION (in other words, the paper of the print or the base layer of a film).

Half-frame. Film format measuring 24 x 18mm (1 x ¾in), half the size of standard format 35mm pictures.

High-key. Picture containing mainly light tones. See also LOW-KEY.

Highlights. Brightest area of the subject. In the negative these are areas of greatest DENSITY.

Holography. Technique whereby information is recorded on a photographic plate as an interference pattern which, when viewed under the appropriate conditions, yields a three-dimensional image. Holography bears little relation to conventional photography except in its use of a light-sensitive film.

Hot-shoe. Accessory plate on a camera for holding a flashgun in position, and incorporating a live contact for firing the flash when the SHUTTER is fired.

Hue. The quality that distinguishes between colours of the same saturation and brightness – the quality, for example, of redness or greenness.

I

Incident light. Light that is falling on the subject. When a subject is being photographed, readings may be taken of the incident light instead of the reflected light.

Infrared radiation. Electromagnetic radiation, having WAVELENGTHS longer than visible red light. Infrared radiation is felt as heat, and can be recorded on special types of photographic film. See also IR SETTING.

Intermittency effect. Phenomenon observed when an EMULSION is given a series of brief EXPOSURES. The DENSITY of the image thus produced is lower than the image density produced by a single exposure equal to the total duration of the short exposures.

Inverse square law. The rule that states that for a point source of light, the intensity of the light decreases with the square of the distance from the source. Thus when the distance from the source is doubled, the light intensity is reduced by a factor of four.

IR (infrared) setting. A mark sometimes found on the focusing ring of a camera indicating the shift in focus needed when using black-and-white infrared film. INFRARED RADIATION is refracted less than visible light, and the infrared image is therefore brought into focus slightly behind the visible one.

ISO. Scale introduced by the International Standards Organization for the measurement of FILM SPEED, which combines the figures previously used in the ASA and DIN scales. The full rating for a medium-speed film is therefore ISO 100/21 – this however is usually abbreviated to ISO 100. The larger the number the faster, and more sensitive, the EMULSION. The scale is arranged so that a film rated at ISO 200 is twice as fast as one rated at ISO 100 – while one rated at ISO 400 is four times as fast.

J

Joule. Unit of energy in the SI (Système International) system of units. The joule is used in photography to indicate the output of an electronic flash.

K

Kelvin (K). Unit used to measure COLOUR TEMPERATURE.

L

Laser. Acronym for Light Amplification by Stimulated Emission of Radiation. Device for producing an intense beam of coherent light that is of a single very pure colour. Used in the production of holograms (see HOLOGRAPHY).

Latensification. Technique used to increase effective film speed by fogging the film, either chemically or with light, between exposure and development.

Latent image. Invisible image recorded on photographic EMULSION after EXPOSURE, but before development by chemicals.

Latitude. Tolerance of photographic material to variations in EXPOSURE.

Lens hood. Simple lens accessory, usually made of rubber or plastic, used to shield the lens from light coming from areas outside the field of view – thus preventing FLARE.

Lith film. A very high-contrast film that is used to eliminate grey tones and reduce the image to areas of pure black or pure white.

Long-focus lens. Lens of focal length greater than that of the STANDARD LENS for a given format. Long-focus lenses have a narrow field of view, and consequently make distant objects appear closer. See also TELEPHOTO LENS.

Low-key. A picture that contains predominantly dark tones. See also HIGH-KEY.

M

Mackie line. Line appearing around a highlight on a silver halide emulsion. It is produced by the lateral diffusion of exhausted developer that causes edge effects. see also SABATTIER EFFECT.

Macro lens. A lens giving an image that is life-size or bigger – a MAGNIFICATION RATIO of 1:1 or greater. The term is generally used to describe any close-focusing lens. Macro lenses can also be used at ordinary subject distances.

Macrophotography. Close-up photography in the range of magnification between life-size and about ten times life-size.

Magnification ratio. Ratio of image size to object size. The magnification ratio is used to judge the capabilities of a MACRO LENS, and can also be useful in calculating the correct EXPOSURE for close-ups.

Masking. Term used to describe ways in which light is prevented from reaching selected areas of an image for various purposes. Some enlargers, for example, incorporate masking devices that cut down stray light passing around the negative or transparency. A masking frame is placed beneath the enlarger lens to establish print size, determine proportions of the picture and keep the paper flat.

Mercury vapour lamp. Type of light source sometimes used in studio photography, giving a bluish light. The light is produced by passing an electric current through a tube filled with mercury vapour.

Microphotography. Technique used to copy documents and similar materials on to a very small-format film, so that a large amount of information may be stored compactly. The term is sometimes also used to refer to the technique of taking photographs through a microscope, otherwise known as PHOTOMICROGRAPHY.

Microprism. Special type of focusing screen composed of a grid of tiny prisms, often incorporated into the standard viewing screens of manual-focus SLR cameras. The microprism gives a fragmented image when the image is out of focus.

Mired. Acronym for micro-reciprocal degree. Unit on a scale of COLOUR

TEMPERATURE used to calibrate COLOUR CORRECTION FILTERS. The mired value of a light is derived by dividing one million by the colour temperature in KELVIN.

Mirror lens. TELEPHOTO lens of a compact design whose construction is based on a combination of lenses and curved mirrors. Light rays from the subject are reflected backward and forward inside the barrel of the lens before reaching the film plane. Also known as a catadioptric lens. Because of its compact design, a mirror lens can be used as a telephoto lens that is smaller and lighter than its traditionally constructed equivalent.

Montage. Composite photographic image made from several different original pictures.

Motor drive. Battery-powered camera feature or accessory used to wind the film on automatically after each shot, and to rewind the film at the end of the roll. A fast motor drive can be used to take several pictures a second, when shooting sport, for example.

N

Negative. Image in which light tones are recorded as dark tones, and vice versa. In colour negatives every colour in the original subject is represented by its complementary colour.

Negative lens. See DIVERGING LENS.

Neutral density filter. A uniformly grey filter that reduces the brightness of an image without altering its colour content. It is used when the light is too bright for the film being used. A graduated ND filter (which is grey at the top and clear at the bottom) is used in landscape photography to reduce contrast between a bright sky and a darker foreground.

Newton's rings. Narrow multi-coloured bands that appear when two transparent surfaces are sandwiched together with imperfect contact. The pattern is caused by interference, and can be troublesome when slides or negatives are held between glass or plastic.

Nodal point. Point of intersection between the optical axis of a compound lens and one of the two principal planes of refraction. A compound lens thus has a front and a rear nodal point from which its basic measurements (such as FOCAL LENGTH) are made.

Normal lens. See STANDARD LENS.

O

Opacity. Objective measurement of the degree of opaqueness of a material; the ratio of incident light to transmitted light.

Open flash. Technique of firing flash manually after the camera SHUTTER has been opened, instead of synchronizing the flash automatically.

Optical axis. Imaginary line through the optical centre of a lens system.

Orthochromatic. Term used to describe black and white EMULSIONS that are insensitive to red light. See also PANCHROMATIC.

P

Pan-and-tilt head. Type of tripod head employing independent locking mechanisms for movement in two planes at right angles to each other. Thus the camera can be locked in one plane while remaining free to move in the other.

Panchromatic. Term used to describe black and white photographic EMULSIONS that are sensitive to all the visible colours (although not necessarily equally to each of them). Nearly all modern films are panchromatic. See also ORTHOCHROMATIC.

Panning. Technique of moving the camera during EXPOSURE to follow a moving subject, giving an impression of

speed. A relatively slow shutter speed is used, so that the background is more blurred than the subject.

Panoramic camera. Any camera that is capable of producing an image whose width is significantly wider than its height. Usually used for landscapes.

Parallax. The difference between what is seen through the VIEWFINDER and what is recorded on the film. It occurs in non-SLR cameras where the viewfinder and the lens have slightly different viewpoints. It becomes a problem when shooting close-ups.

Pentaprism. Five-sided prism used in the construction of eye-level viewfinders for SLR cameras, which ensures that the image seen in the viewfinder is the right way round and the right way up. In practice the pentaprism often has more than five sides, as unnecessary parts of the prism are cut off to reduce its bulk.

Permanence. Permanence is determined initially by the effectiveness of the processing, and in colour photographs by the stability of the dyes in the emulsion layers. Development and fixing must be followed by thorough washing to remove all traces of those residual silver compounds that could affect the image's appearance. If prints are to be mounted, dry mounting is the most permanent method because it does not introduce any potentially harmful chemicals to the back of the print, as do many glues. When processed and stored carefully, black-and-white photographic materials will generally stay in good condition indefinitely. Colour images are less permanent, and are especially susceptible to direct sunlight. For maximum life expectancy, colour images should be stored in refrigerated conditions or as separation negatives.

Photoelectric cell. Light-sensitive cell used in the circuit of a light meter. Some types of photoelectric cell generate an electric current when stimulated by light, others react by a change in their electrical resistance.

Photoflood. Bright tungsten filament bulb used as an artificial light source in photography. The bulb is over-run (to increase the brightness, more current passes through the filament than would in a standard bulb running for a longer period) and it therefore has a short life.

Photometer. Instrument for measuring the intensity of light by comparing it with a standard source.

Photomicrography. The technique of taking photographs through the lens of a microscope.

Pinhole camera. Simple camera that employs a very small hole instead of a lens to form an image.

Polarized light. Light whose electrical vibrations are confined to a single plane. In everyday conditions, light is usually unpolarized, having electrical (and magnetic) vibrations in every plane. Light reflected from shiny non-metallic surfaces is usually polarized and can be controlled using a POLARIZING FILTER.

Polarizing filters. Thin, transparent filters used as a lens accessory to cut down reflections from certain shiny surfaces (such as glass and water), or to intensify the colour of a blue sky (by reducing the amount of light reflected by the sky). Rotating the filter will vary the proportion of the polarized light that is blocked. There are two types of polarizing filter – linear and circular. Circular polarizing filters are constructed in a different way from linear polarizers so that they do not interfere with the exposure and autofocus systems of some cameras, and are therefore necessary when using autofocus SLRs.

Positive. Image in which the light tones correspond to the light areas of the subject, and the dark tones to the dark areas. In colour photography, it refers to an image in which the colours correspond to those of the original subject. See NEGATIVE.

Positive lens. See CONVERGING LENS.

Posterization. Technique of drastically simplifying the tones of an image by making several negatives from an original each with different densities and contrasts, and then sandwiching them together and printing them in register. The effect can also be achieved electronically.

Primary colours. Red, green and blue light. These can be mixed together to give white light, or in different proportions to give light of any other colour.

Process film. Slow, fine-grained film of good resolving power that is used for copying work.

Process lens. Highly corrected lens designed specially for copying work.

Pushing. Technique that increases the effective SPEED of a film by extending its normal development time.

R

Rangefinder. Optical device for measuring distance, sometimes coupled to the focusing system of a camera lens. A rangefinder displays two images, showing the scene from slightly different viewpoints, that must be superimposed one on the other to establish the subject's distance.

Real image. In optics, the term used to describe an image that can be formed on a screen, as distinct from a VIRTUAL IMAGE. The rays of light actually pass through the image before entering the eye of the observer.

Reciprocity law. Principle according to which the DENSITY of the image formed when the EMULSION is developed is directly proportional to the duration of the EXPOSURE and the intensity of the light. However, with extremely short or long exposures, and with unusual light intensities, the law fails, leading to unpredictable results – hence the term reciprocity failure. See also INTERMITTENCY EFFECT.

Reflector. Sheets of white, gold or silver material employed to reflect light into shadow areas.

Reflex camera. Generic name for types of camera whose viewing systems employ a mirror to reflect an image onto the viewfinder screen. See TWIN-LENS REFLEX and SINGLE-LENS REFLEX.

Refraction. Bending of a ray of light travelling obliquely from one medium to another; the ray is refracted at the surface of the two media.

Resin-coated (RC) paper. Photographic printing paper coated with a synthetic resin to prevent the paper base from absorbing liquids during processing. Resin-coated papers can be washed and dried more quickly than untreated papers can.

Resolving power. Ability of an optical system (or an EMULSION) to distinguish between objects that are positioned very close together.

Retina. Light-sensitive layer at the back of the eye.

Reversal film. Photographic film that gives a positive image when processed. A film intended for producing slides, rather than negatives.

Reversing ring. Camera accessory that enables the lens to be attached back to front. Used in close-up photography to achieve a high magnification ratio.

Ring flash. Type of electronic flash unit that fits around the lens to produce flat, shadowless lighting. It is particularly useful in close-up work.

Rising front. One of the principal forms of CAMERA MOVEMENT. The lens is moved vertically in a plane parallel to the film. This mechanism is particularly important in architectural photography, as it allows the photographer to include the top of the building in a photograph without causing CONVERGING VERTICALS to appear.

S

Sabattier effect. Partial reversal of the tones of a photographic image resulting from a secondary EXPOSURE to light during development. Sometimes also know as SOLARIZATION or, more correctly, pseudo-solarization. A special effect usually carried out during the printing stage.

Sandwiching. The projection or printing of two or more negatives or slides together to produce a composite image.

Saturated colour. Pure colour, free from any mixture with grey.

Selenium cell. One of the principal types of photoelectric cell used in light meters. A selenium cell produces a current when stimulated by light, proportional to the intensity of the light.

Separation negative. A negative that records one of the three primary colours of a subject, or, more usually, of a transparency, as a silver image. For photomechanical printing processes a set of three separation negatives is produced, recording the red, green and blue components respectively, together with a negative recording the tones of the whole scene. These are used to produce four plates in cyan, magenta, yellow and black.

Shutter. Camera mechanism that controls the duration of the EXPOSURE. The two main types of shutter are the BETWEEN-THE-LENS SHUTTER and the FOCAL-PLANE SHUTTER.

Single-lens reflex (SLR). One of the most popular types of camera design. Its name derives from its viewfinder system, which enables the user to see an image that is produced by the same lens as the one used for taking the photograph. A hinged mirror reflects this image onto a viewing screen, where the picture may be composed and focused. When the SHUTTER is released the mirror flips out of the light path, so that the film can be exposed. See also TWIN-LENS REFLEX.

Slave unit. Photoelectric device used to trigger electronic flash units in studio work. The slave unit detects light from a primary flashgun linked directly to the camera, and fires the secondary flash unit to which it is connected.

SLR. Abbreviation for SINGLE-LENS REFLEX.

Snoot. Conical lamp attachment used to control the beam of a studio light.

Soft focus. Slight diffusion of the image achieved by use of a special FILTER or similar means, which softens the definition of the image. The effect is usually used to give a romantic haze to a photograph.

Solarization. Strictly, the complete or partial reversal of the tones of an image as a result of extreme overexposure. Often used to refer to the SABATTIER EFFECT, which produces results similar in appearance.

Spectrum. The multi-coloured band obtained when light is split up into its component WAVELENGTHS, as when a prism is used to split white light into coloured rays, the term may also refer to the complete range of electromagnetic radiation, extending from the shortest to the longest wavelengths and including visible light.

Speed. The sensitivity of an EMULSION to light. See ISO and FILM SPEED.

Spherical aberration. Lens defect resulting in an image that is not sharp, caused by light rays passing through the outer edges of a lens being more strongly refracted than those passing through the central parts. Not all rays, therefore, are brought to exactly the same focus.

Spot meter. Special light meter that takes a reading from a very narrow ANGLE OF VIEW. In some TTL METERS the reading may be taken from only a small central portion of the image in the VIEWFINDER.

Standard lens. Lens of FOCAL LENGTH approximately equal to the diagonal of the negative format for which it is intended. In the case of 35mm cameras the standard lens is a 50mm, for the 6 x 6cm (2¼ x 2¼ in) format it is an 80mm lens.

Stop. Alternative name for an APERTURE setting, or F NUMBER.

Stopping down. Term used for reducing the APERTURE of a lens.

Subminiature camera. Camera using 16mm film to take negatives measuring 12 x 17mm (½ x ¾in).

Supplementary lens. Simple POSITIVE LENS used as an accessory for close-ups. The supplementary lens fits over the normal lens, producing a slightly magnified image.

T

Telephoto. Lens (or lens setting) with a long FOCAL LENGTH and a small ANGLE OF VIEW.

Test strip. Print showing the effects of several trial EXPOSURE times, made in the darkroom to assess the correct exposure time.

TLR. See TWIN-LENS REFLEX camera.

Transparency. A photograph viewed by transmitted, rather than reflected, light. When mounted in a rigid frame, the transparency is called a slide.

T setting. Abbreviation of time setting. A setting available on some cameras for giving very long EXPOSURES. When the SHUTTER release is pressed, the shutter remains open until the release is pressed a second time. See also B SETTING.

TTL meter. Through-the-lens meter. Built-in EXPOSURE meter that measures the intensity of light in the image produced by the main camera lens. Principally found in SINGLE-LENS REFLEX cameras.

Twin-lens reflex (TLR) camera. Type of camera whose viewing system employs a secondary lens of FOCAL LENGTH equal to that of the main 'taking' lens. A fixed mirror reflects the image from the viewing lens up onto a ground glass screen. Twin-lens reflex cameras can suffer badly from PARALLAX error, particularly when focused at close distances. See also SINGLE-LENS REFLEX camera.

U

Ultraviolet radiation. Electromagnetic radiation of WAVELENGTHS shorter than those of violet light (which is the shortest visible wavelength). They affect most photographic emulsions to some extent. See also INFRARED RADIATION.

Uprating. See PUSHING.

UV filter. Filter used over the camera lens to absorb ultraviolet radiation. Haze scatters ultraviolet light, so pictures taken on hazy days through a UV filter will be clearer than those taken without.

V

Variable contrast (VC) paper.
Photographic printing paper sensitized to give a range of different contrast grades, each activated by a different coloured filter in the enlarger. The best-known variable contrast paper is Ilford's Multigrade.

View camera. Large-format studio camera whose viewing system consists of a ground glass screen at the back of the camera on which the picture is composed and focused before the film is inserted. The front and back of the camera are attached by a flexible BELLOWS unit, which allows a full range of CAMERA MOVEMENTS.

Viewfinder. Window or frame on a camera showing the scene that will appear in the picture.

Vignette. Picture printed in such a way that the image fades gradually into the border area.

Virtual image. In optics, an image that cannot be obtained on a screen; a virtual image is seen by an observer in a position through which rays of light appear to have passed, but in fact have not. See also REAL IMAGE.

W

Wavelength. The distance between successive points of equal 'phase' on a lightwave; the distance, for example, between successive crests or troughs.

Wide-angle lens. Lens of FOCAL LENGTH shorter than that of a standard lens. A wide-angle lens, or lens setting, has a short focal length and a wide ANGLE OF VIEW.

X

X-rays. Electromagnetic radiation with WAVELENGTHS very much shorter than those of visible light.

Z

Zone focusing. A technique of presetting the APERTURE and focusing of the camera so that the entire zone in which the subject is likely to appear is covered by the DEPTH OF FIELD. This technique is particularly useful in such areas of photography as sport and photojournalism in which there is not enough time to focus the camera more accurately at the actual moment of taking the photograph.

Zone system. System of relating EXPOSURE readings to tonal values in picture-taking, development and printing, popularized by the American landscape photographer Ansel Adams.

Zoom lens. Lens with a variable FOCAL LENGTH, where the FOCAL PLANE remains unchanged while the focal length is being altered.

Index

Page numbers in **bold** type refer to main entries.